PRAISE FOR *100 PROVEN WAYS TO ACQUIRE AND KEEP CLIENTS FOR LIFE*

"Richard says, 'Relationships drive revenue. Build them and you will soar.' If one has any doubts about the truth of this statement, I'd ask them to read this magnificent book. Buckle your seatbelt, dear reader. You are about to take a very abundant ride."

—Bob Burg, coauthor of the international bestseller, *The Go-Giver*, and author of the sales classic, *Endless Referrals*

"Richard nails it in his new book! Not only does Richard provide valuable insights, like only he can do; he also provides important implementation strategies. If you are interested in Rock Solid Relationships, this book is a must read!!"

—Harry P. Hoopis, chief executive officer at Hoopis Performance Network and recipient of the 2022 John Newton Russell Memorial Award

"I expected a great book, but this prolific book has really outperformed Richard's previous works. This book should be used as your Bible for customer relationship strategies and tactics. With *100 Proven Ways to Acquire and Keep Clients for Life*, your luck will be augmented dramatically with great skill."

—Milton Pedraza, CEO of Luxury Institute, LLC

"I have known Richard for almost thirty years! He trained me when I was a brand-new agent. The proven, actionable tactics he shares in this book can set your entire career on a new trajectory and will bring you permanent business success."

—Tom Hegna, retirement expert, economist, bestselling author, and international speaker

"Richard Weylman's book is a powerhouse of actionable strategies tailored for client acquisition and retention. It's an excellent blueprint to follow for cultivating enduring client relationships. Real-life examples bring these strategies to life, making them accessible and adaptable across industries. A must-read for professionals striving to excel in client-centric businesses."

—Adrienne Lally and Attilio Leonardi, co-owners of Team Lally, Keller Williams Honolulu

"Richard Weylman has always been ahead of common thinking. He has always focused on what is effective and to do that which others can't do, won't do, or haven't thought of yet. He understands the human emotional components that are the true differentiators. I have been in financial services for fifty years and, if I were you, I would get this book and read it!"

—Joe Jordan, author of *Living a Life of Significance* and recipient of the 2023 John Newton Russell Memorial Award

"Every reader, including me, will see themselves and the professionals they work with in this book and know how to be better immediately."

—Jim Ruta, president of Advisorcraft Media

"This book brilliantly captures the essence of choosing the pain of discipline over the pain of regret, reminding us that every challenge we face only makes us more unstoppable in the future. By this book's teachings, we can develop a portfolio of clients that will last a lifetime!"

—Louis David Spagnuolo, chairman of the board, PrivateJet.com

"What makes Richard and this book really special is his ability to teach others how to use their 'own voice,' to help us authentically connect with the lifeblood of our businesses… our clients."

—Colin C Lake, CIMA® founder/president of Developing the Next Leaders

"A must-read book! Richard Weylman shares with you the secrets of how to engage and insight on how to keep a client for life. He has inspired me with simple yet powerful, proven techniques to use every day to be successful in my business."

—Shirley Luu, founder and CEO of Shirley Luu & Associate (with more than 27,500 clients served!)

"I just finished reading and re-reading my advance copy of '100 Proven Ways To Acquire & Keep Clients For Life' by Richard Weylman. His depth of experience continues to surpass what he has written previously. This is not just a 30,000-foot overview, but Weylman delivers the specific tactics for successful customer relationship sales and marketing. This is a Must Read! "

—Jim Ziegler, CSP, HSG, OG President @ ZIEGLER SUPERSYSTEMS, Inc. #AlphaDawg

100

PROVEN WAYS TO

ACQUIRE AND KEEP CLIENTS FOR LIFE

Also by C. Richard Weylman

Opening Closed Doors: Keys to Reaching Hard-to-Reach People

The Power of Why: Breaking Out in a Competitive Marketplace

Endless Prospects: 301 Tactics to Reach Hard-to-Reach People

100

PROVEN WAYS TO

ACQUIRE AND KEEP CLIENTS FOR LIFE

The Path to Permanent Business Success

Richard WEYLMAN

mango
PUBLISHING

CORAL GABLES

For permission requests, please contact the publisher at:
Mango Publishing Group
2850 S Douglas Road, 2nd Floor
Coral Gables, FL 33134 USA
info@mango.bz

For special orders, quantity sales, course adoptions and corporate sales, please email the publisher at sales@mango.bz. For trade and wholesale sales, please contact Ingram Publisher Services at customer.service@ingramcontent.com or +1.800.509.4887.

100 Proven Ways to Acquire and Keep Clients for Life: The Path to Permanent Business Success

Library of Congress Cataloging-in-Publication number: 2023949532
ISBN: (p) 978-1-68481-524-1, (e) 978-1-68481-525-8
BISAC category code: BUS018000, BUSINESS & ECONOMICS / Customer Relations

Dedicated to those who want to achieve permanent
business success and leave a lasting legacy.

TABLE OF CONTENTS

FOREWORD

Imagine one Christmas, as a twelve-year-old orphan being shuttled through the foster care system, your current foster family drops you off with a neighbor because only "real family members" are invited on the Christmas holiday trip. Then, instead of getting to celebrate with this "drop off family," you are sent to the basement (by yourself!) to sleep and spend the ten days while the family enjoys the festivities upstairs.

The fright and loneliness this little boy must have experienced is difficult to even fathom. Personally, I cannot imagine a more horrible "relationship" experience than this.

And yet, the author of this book, Richard Weylman—an icon in the world of customer and client experiences, considered by many to be *the* leading authority on a subject where *relationships* are paramount to success—began his life living through some of the worst relationship ordeals imaginable.

Not only did the author overcome this unfortunate aspect of his life...he used it as a springboard to launch a revolution in how the best companies and most successful individual professionals, regardless of their role, view the "total client experience."

One could even say that he's taken this very paradigm to an entirely new level.

Richard Weylman teaches that, "Thoughtfulness, empathy, caring, and kindness are valuable relationship-building traits that no amount of competitor marketing dollars can defeat."

Richard has championed this type of relationship as a General Sales Manager and executive in the luxury automotive industry, and as the former head of sales and marketing for *The Robb Report*, a luxury lifestyle magazine.

And now, for more than thirty years, he has equipped major corporations and individual sales and service professionals to create client experiences that have brought substantial increases in acquisition and retention.

These increases significantly boost sales and wallet share, improve cross-selling efforts, lower the cost of acquisition of new business, and increase the lifetime value of the client relationship, with an immediate and sustainable impact on the bottom line.

Richard has worked with companies and their teams in many industries, including financial, fast casual dining, professional sports teams, home services, direct sales, franchising, and hospitality, just to name a few. He has shown them all that great experiences are *not* just for the luxury consumer but can impact every prospect and client regardless of the product or service being sold.

It can be said that people will go out of their way to be in relationship with, do business with, and tell the world about the sales and service professionals and companies who will provide those experiences.

So, how has Richard made such a difference with his clients?

By helping them develop a culture that conveys a warm, wonderful, and fantastic experience at every...single...touchpoint.

The exact right words can often make the difference between a good relationship and a powerful, bonded relationship that results in new client acquisition and word of mouth (what we at our company call "personal walking ambassadors") that will take your business to great heights.

As you read, pay close attention to the many times Richard suggests using a certain word or phrase rather than others more commonly used. These subtle differences are likely to result in powerful emotional connections. Then make those new words and phrases—and this is *so key*—part of your company and/or personal culture.

Many of Richard's tactics will seem so simple to apply that you might wonder, "Of course, why didn't I think of that?" The key, though, is understanding that each of these "seemingly simple" tactics is based on a much larger and very specific principle: that truly caring about the other person and their needs, their wants, their desires (and yes, their problems and challenges) is where each of these life-affirming and powerful actions actually originate.

As Richard says, "Relationships drive revenue. Build them and you will soar." If anyone has any doubts about the truth of this statement, I'd ask them to read (actually, study) this magnificent book, apply its principles and suggestions, and experience the increase in their income that they will have well-deserved.

Once you understand the "why-to" and learn the "how-to," you and your business will become absolutely unstoppable. Buckle your seatbelt, dear reader. You are about to take a very abundant ride.

My recommendation to you as a reader and fellow learner: This is a book you won't want to read just once, but rather many times in order to truly take in its essence as well as its many specific tactics and ideas. It'll also make an excellent resource guide so keep it at an easily reachable distance, perhaps even on a corner of your desk. You *will* find yourself coming back to it time and again.

If you lead an organization, consider putting a copy of this invaluable resource in the hands of each of your team members and watch how a company culture of this type of excellence helps leverage the value you provide to your clients.

And then purchase the book for the young up-and-comers in your life (children, grandchildren, protégés) whom you'd like to equip for their present and future, and set up to be nine steps ahead of the game…in a ten-step game.

WOW! THANK YOU, RICHARD WEYLMAN, FOR SHARING YOUR MASTERY AND MAGNIFICENCE WITH US, BOTH THROUGH YOUR MANY YEARS OF TEACHING, AND NOW IN YOUR LATEST GEM OF A BOOK!

—BOB BURG, COAUTHOR OF THE INTERNATIONAL BESTSELLER, *THE GO-GIVER*, AND AUTHOR OF THE SALES CLASSIC, *ENDLESS REFERRALS*

INTRODUCTION

WHY INVEST YOUR TIME?

Recently, I was speaking at a conference in Nashville, TN, on *"How You Can Stand Apart from the Competition."*

I reiterated a story I had read on LinkedIn that day by a woman who had a standing order with Chewy, an online pet food retailer, for her cat's food.

She received her monthly order, but sadly the cat had recently died. She called Chewy's customer service to return the cat food and was told, *"Please donate it to your shelter instead and we will give you a full credit."* Nice!

But the story doesn't end there. She went on to write that a few days after her call she received a bouquet of flowers and a sympathy card from the customer service rep at Chewy!

As soon as I told the story, a woman in the audience yelled out, *"That was my cat!"* I had no idea she was in the audience.

I then asked the audience, *"What do you think about what that person at Chewy did?"* They started chanting, *"We're switching to Chewy! We're switching to Chewy!"*

The thoughtfulness that a person at Chewy demonstrated moved a ballroom full of people.

Read that again: It was a person at Chewy who was thoughtful and caring. Not some computer program or IT call, data scan, or AI interpretation with its predetermined action.

No, it was a person. A person committed to elevating the experience, and the emotional connection, for the relationship that client had with Chewy. As a result, some will read and hear what this person did and actually switch their business to Chewy.

Some will read this and say, "Well, Chewy is a big company and they can do that. Besides, it is part of their culture to engage with their clients emotionally and they are known for that. I am too busy and don't have time for *that* stuff."

You are not "too busy," and it is not about having time. It's a matter of having your strategic priorities in order to keep the business you have and acquire even more.

Whether you call the people with whom you do business clients or customers, in the end they are people. Real people.

With the ongoing commoditization of products and services, people have many choices about where to spend or invest their money. As a result, they are constantly evaluating whether they are with the right professional and the right company. They ask themselves, "Do I feel appreciated and cared for? Am I consistently treated with thoughtfulness, kindness, and empathy?"

This great reevaluation by consumers requires professionals and companies to reset their thinking and consequently their actions. How much business would you acquire if you were known for your thoughtfulness, kindness, caring, and empathy?

You may think, as so many do, that your clients are satisfied with what you offer and do for them. You might think you are doing a good job for them and that they would never fire you.

Many companies are so invested in this thinking that they even survey their clients and rely on their "satisfaction scores" as a measure of how well the company is doing. What these companies fail to realize is that satisfaction scores only look backward. They lull sales, service, and marketing professionals and company leaders to sleep instead of motivating them to do more.

Moreover, most surveys do not gather first-person tactical data from buyers on how to elevate and better their experience in the future so that they will actually stay with the company. Or if they do gather data, it is so general or ethereal as to be non-actionable and is archived as "feedback."

In the real world, people's expectations and desires have evolved significantly. As the chair of a consulting and coaching firm, our ongoing years of research and direct experience with consumers demonstrates that at least 20 to 30 percent of those "satisfied" clients are actually "loyalty neutral" at any given time.

Before you ask if this is possible, consider that you prove it repeatedly whenever you bring in a new client whose previous professional and their company are puzzled that their "satisfied" customer left them.

The cost of client acquisition is capital-intensive, time-consuming, and requires relentless effort. Consequently, your focus—regardless of your role in the business—should be to turn every "satisfied" client into a delighted advocate of your business. Delighted advocates tell others, and this substantial word of mouth helps you acquire more clients just like them.

In this book, I will describe what people are looking for today from the professionals and companies with whom they do business. More importantly, I will detail what you need to do to meet their expectations to keep their business and to acquire more clients like them.

You will see, step by step, tactic by tactic, exactly how you can deliver on your clients' and prospects' expectations and solidify their relationship with you. The tactics offered in this book are proven ways to create a community of delighted advocates and a highly profitable and sustainable business. To that end, as you read, it will serve you well to take note of the tactics you can use in your own business.

I have spent years researching and engaging with the clients of companies in a variety of industries, including luxury goods, finance, insurance, travel, professional sports teams, fast casual dining, automotive, hospitality, direct sales, and many more. This lifetime of engaging with many thousands of people has been a gift.

It is a gift that I am sharing with you here, as it has enabled me to identify what people really want from you and how you can deliver it.

And believe me, if they don't get it from you and your business, they *will* fire you and find someone who will give it to them. However, if you give people what they really want, they will be your best source of new business growth.

Maya Angelou has been credited with saying, *"I've learned that people will forget what you said, people will forget what you did, but people will never forget how you made them feel."*

Enjoy the read and the outcome that will result if you follow the advice in this book. There is real value when you become the most-loved professional and company in your area.

However, to be crystal clear, this is not the last word on this topic.

That word belongs to your clients, who will be delighted to advocate for you based on what you learn and implement from this book.

CHAPTER 1

WHAT CLIENTS AND PROSPECTS WANT AND WHY YOU GET FIRED WITHOUT IT

Most professionals and their companies are focused on and love the products or services they sell and service. That is understandable. Enjoying and having passion for what you create, sell, or provide is critical for success in any business today.

However, while you may love your *products and services*, the client is focused on, and cherishes, the *experiences* they have with you and your company.

Unfortunately, most professionals and companies do not realize the significance of the client (or prospect) experience, nor the need to consistently elevate it over their products and services.

A person's experience with you, your team, and your company affects their perception of your value and ultimately their loyalty to you.

Make no mistake, the elevated experience consumers seek now is far more than just delivering good service. Good service is a minimum expectation of all consumers today. If good service is good enough to retain a client, then why are people changing companies and professionals?

As an example, in Engati Digital's recent survey of a hundred top advisors (known for giving great service) in the financial industry, 81 percent said client retention was now more important to them than client acquisition post-pandemic. They know that good or great service alone will not keep business on the books.

With very few exceptions, people have multiple choices when looking for a company or sales professional. While the purchase of a product or service is often perceived and functions as a "transaction," it is the experience that people have around that purchase, and thereafter, that captures their ongoing spending and their loyalty.

Dozens of studies have been conducted by organizations such as US Luxury Institute, PwC Research, Reuters, Pew Research, and Zendesk that clearly illustrate that people today are far more loyal to the experience they have and the resulting sense of relationship than they are to a product or a brand.

In just one example of many, in a recent study conducted by PwC Research's Professional Services Group, 80 percent of respondents indicated that both real *and* perceived value is largely based upon their experience with the professional and by extension the company. It is an integral part of their received value equation.

You inherently know this based on your own purchase and loyalty behavior.

> For example, you might stop going to a noisy restaurant despite the great food and service. If you stop and think about this, you will quickly realize that even when a brand is great in every expected way, one bad experience—like dining in a restaurant that is too noisy to have a conversation—can outweigh all the positives. So, given that value today is not just about product, pricing, and service but also the overall experience, you would probably decide to go somewhere else for dinner.

As another example, think of a financial professional you have engaged. Even if their expertise is clear, their attitude, or their condescending tone, or their lack of personalization could easily lead you to question, Am I in the right place with the right professional?

Or consider the repair technician who didn't show up at the appointed time, then didn't have the parts needed to do the repair and said you would have to call the shop to get rescheduled.

Or the call you made to an online retailer to get an issue resolved or a question answered, only to get the run around.

You don't need me to list more unpleasant experience examples— we all have had them and continue to have them, and as a result those professionals and their companies have lost our business.

In the introduction, I wrote about how "satisfied" individuals are loyalty neutral. You prove this repeatedly when you capture new business by moving a client from their current professional and firm to your business.

People today are not just buying the product or service you are selling. People are buying the experience they have with you and the relationship and emotional bond that it fosters.

Client experiences also affect the perception and decisions of others more than you know. Client socializing and social media have become the true centers for influence, not just of influence.

In this digital social media world, Zendesk studies have shown that up to 87 percent of clients share good and bad experiences with others. Like it or not, shared experiences of every kind become linked to you and your "brand."

Regardless of whether your business is large or small, when clients do business with and work with you, your name is on the experience they have, and you own it.

And like it or not, every single client and prospective client will have an experience with you, and you get the privilege of deciding what that experience will be.

People have so many choices that the crucial cornerstone of a sustainable, growing, and profitable business is unquestionably the elevation of every client's and prospect's experience. And to make this even more of a burning platform issue that must be addressed, some clients will leave a brand, a professional, or a firm after just a single bad experience!

When you consistently elevate the client's experience, you will build a strong relationship with them, and those relationships will drive ongoing revenue.

Furthermore, the buying population has moved well beyond the often-used phraseology of corporate speak around this topic.

Phrases such as *"client-centric"* and *"customer-focused"* enjoy widespread use. However, they are typically addressed and demonstrated by efforts to *"smooth out"* the so-called *"client's/customer's journey"* by using technology, improving responsiveness, and other strategies.

I suggest a reset of this thinking and lexicon. Thinking of the customer or client as being on a journey may imply that the journey has an ending. God forbid it has an ending, given the lifetime value of a client relationship! It is alarming how few people in business understand, or perhaps more accurately realize or calculate, the lifetime value of a client and how critical their retention is.

WHAT EXPERIENCE DO PEOPLE WANT AND HOW DO THEY DEFINE IT?

People seek an experience with you that is far more personalized and humanized than smoothing out transaction rough spots or giving responsive service. While those things are important, what is most important in this ultra-competitive environment is very clear if you ask them.

Through our consulting work in many industries interviewing clients and customers of widely diverse companies, what people want and how they define an elevated experience has been consistent.

At the core, people today want a level of personal engagement that is not happenstance or just some magical fairy dusting of special offers made by marketing. While loyalty programs and preferred pricing and offers have proven to be useful, what people seek now is far more and deeper than that.

They seek a relationship with you and your company.

They want to feel they are part of your community—a community that you respect and appreciate.

What they seek is an experience that is: *consistently thoughtful, kind, empathetic, and caring, with interactions and moments that create invaluable lasting impressions.*

Large companies balk at this and say, "Well, frontline workers can't be expected to gather information and demonstrate that for customers or clients, as that slows down the service and transaction process."

Others who do much of their business online say that personal engagement and being thoughtful, kind, empathetic, and caring is difficult if not impossible, even with AI and upgraded chat. Yet Amazon and even Walmart and Target have demonstrated that online interactions can still be personalized and elevated.

And it is not just large companies and online providers that balk—individuals and small firms do as well. They, too, are so focused on their products, processes, platforms, plans, and positioning that they do not realize they need to be focused on the one thing that will sustain and grow any and every business: treating prospects, clients, and customers as individual *people*.

Their merchandising mindset is exactly the problem and the reason they can't see the way forward. Even when companies and professionals see themselves as relational, this focus equates to a transaction mindset. This merchandising mindset and lack of awareness eventually lead to the loss of clients and potential ongoing revenues.

Unfortunately, some merchandisers will refuse to change. They will continue to believe their product or service will keep them in transactions with clients. However, they will learn from their own painful experience why the client is the *final* arbiter of loyalty.

Once some of their best clients have left, revenue slumps, and they're in business repair or resuscitation mode, they will then have the time to reconsider and finally focus on their remaining clients as "people."

Make no mistake, Chewy thrives, as does Amazon, Airbnb, The Ritz-Carlton, Freddy's Frozen Custard and Steakburgers, Chick-fil-A, Wynn Resorts, and many, many others, because their professionals take a personal interest in knowing how to elevate their clients' experience. They are laser-focused on developing a relationship with clients and a client experience that develops true advocacy for their brand which results in even more business.

As Jeff Bezos reportedly said, *"We see our customers as invited guests to a party, and we are the hosts. It's our job every day to make every important aspect of the customer experience a little bit better."*

As far back as 1999, this was his focus. When asked, *"Are you a pure internet play?"* he replied, *"Internet, shminternet—what matters is we are solely focused on the customer experience."*

His answer was very telling and serves as a signpost for all of us. While Bezos is not the final arbiter of the customer experience, his answer was part of the beginning of what is unmistakably the experience revolution.

Others have noted the importance of elevating the client experience and the resultant loyal relationship. They offer similar insights.

For example, in a 2018 interview with *Vanity Fair*, Mark Cuban brilliantly said, *"One of the most underrated skills in business right now is being nice."*

Sibel Terhaar, author and critically acclaimed Kindness Activist, said, *"Kindness is more valuable than your job title. People won't remember your job title, but they will remember your kindness."*

Bestselling author Steven Covey said, *"When you show deep empathy toward others, their defensive energy goes down, and positive energy replaces it. That's when you can get more creative in solving problems."*

Regardless of what you are currently doing or how you perceive the strength of your prospect and client relationships, be mindful that consumer expectations are continually evolving.

VALUE TODAY IS SOLELY DEFINED BY THE CONSUMER AND BASED UPON EVERY TOUCHPOINT THEY HAVE WITH YOU, YOUR TEAM, AND YOUR COMPANY.

When you continually elevate their experience through your actions, the results are nothing short of remarkable.

As a research-based consulting firm, we have been blessed to capture the input both before and after an elevated experience becomes *the* strategy for client retention and growth.

People have said that their professional's consistent ongoing interactions that demonstrate thoughtfulness, kindness, empathy, and caring motivate them to be grateful, delighted advocates for the professional and their offerings. *Wow!*

Specifically, those we interviewed across many industries said about their professional:

1. **They feel a deeper emotional connection with you.** They feel that no matter what, they can count on you for the direction and advice they need in your area of expertise. This finding is solid gold.

2. **They feel their relationship with you is strengthened.** They feel as though they are significant to you and to your company instead of just another buyer of your product or services. Most importantly, they said they feel secure that you will be there for them when needed.

3. **They feel motivated to do more business with you.** They feel comfortable with you because they feel you have taken the time to know them and understand them at a deeper level. As a result, they don't feel *any* desire or need to shop around.

4. **They feel it makes you distinct from others.** They feel that your efforts to relate to them and know them sets you apart from those who are stuck in and reliant on the transactional past.

5. **They will advocate for you and what you do for them.** They feel that many could benefit from working with you because you make them feel valued. *Specifically, they feel people they know in their network should know you and would benefit from you and your work.*

These findings illustrate how you will be able to withstand the competitive pressure from other professionals and firms that attack your client base and even the technology offered by chatbots, AI virtual assistants, and ongoing tech innovation.

HOW IS THIS POSSIBLE?

The answer is that by focusing on the experiential, relational side of the business, you will be able to orchestrate your client and prospect interactions in many media.

However, to move forward successfully requires an adjustment. You can no longer think just as a merchandiser—just a plan processor, a product advocate, a process devotee, or a provider. Rather, you must adjust to focusing on and thinking about every current and prospective client as a *person*.

Not a transaction, not a buyer, but a person who, when treated with thoughtfulness, kindness, empathy, and caring, will become an advocate for your brand.

Does this mean everyone will respond to your efforts to elevate their experience and build a relationship with you? No. But then, do you really want to do business with people who don't value those traits?

That said, most people almost desperately want to feel appreciated and connected. However, given their many choices, they are both discerning and quick to judge.

Asking your new clients why they left their previous professional and firm provides actionable insight.

The important question is not *"Why did you join us?"* but rather *"Why did you leave them?"*

Understanding this gives you real insight into their expectations as well as the competitive messaging you can use. Their answers will illustrate the remarkable opportunity you have to win more business by consistently elevating every client relationship and consequently bonding with them emotionally.

Here are a few of the answers our clients have heard when they asked their new customer, *"Why did you leave the professional or company you were with?"*

- *We didn't feel a sense of connection.*

- *We didn't feel welcome, and they weren't nice.*

- *We didn't have a sense we were anything more than a buyer to them.*

- *We felt like they were just going through the motions and showing us property above our price range.*

- *They always had their agenda with no consideration for what we really needed as a couple.*

- *We got tired of not getting regular updates.*

- *They were so into themselves; they were always talking at me.*

- *They always said how busy they were, and we felt rushed. We finally decided they were too busy for us.*

- And the worst in my view was: *They were rude to my wife.*

Some of you might say that these are just sales training and presentation issues. I disagree. The problem is less about sales training and more about how prospects and even clients are not being graciously treated as people.

However, this book is not about focusing on what you or anyone else is doing wrong. Rather, it is about focusing on what you can do better.

When you solidify your relationships with clients and prospective clients by elevating their experience with you, it engages them emotionally, and they will know unequivocally they are in the right place with the right professional.

Here is an example sent to me by an audience member after I spoke at a conference he attended. Only the names, occupations, and location are omitted for his and his client's privacy.

Richard, I loved what you had to say at the summer conference and really started to think about how I could "elevate the client experience to stand apart from the competition."

So, I had a meeting with a young professional yesterday morning for whom I recently did a financial plan. She was bringing in her father-in-law to essentially listen in and critique. He's the owner of the firm she works in and the patriarch of the family. I thought I would take some of your advice and elevate this early morning meeting with some fresh-baked pastries on a nice tray and serve them on small plates.

I went to Target the night before and bought a full place setting set with silverware. It was over seventy dollars, and this box was HEAVY. I take it home and wash everything for the next day. Then here I am, at eight in the morning, in a full suit, lugging a huge box out to my car. I stop and buy an assortment of fresh French pastries and drive to the office. Now I'm lugging my bag, a box of plates, and a box of pastries across a parking lot. I get in, unpack everything, and set the table. At this point I am sweating and thinking to myself, "What am I doing? If this doesn't work, Weylman owes me a hundred bucks!"

Clients arrive, I greet them and tell them I brought in fresh French pastries. Richard, I kid you not, they both said, "We appreciate you for being so thoughtful," and then dove into those pastries like they had never had any before!

I end up signing the father-in-law up for a plan AND he wants to "consolidate" all his investable assets with us! I'm bringing my plate set and fresh pastries to every meeting now. Thanks for the inspiration!

I was impressed with his commitment to implementation on apparently very short notice.

WHERE DO YOU GO FROM HERE?

Throughout the remaining chapters, I will detail for you the tactics *that people have said* increase their perception that you are thoughtful, kind, empathetic, and caring toward them. These actions will result in you standing apart from the competition and being a valued professional.

They will deliver the four Es—an Elevated Experience that creates Emotional Engagement and the relationship people seek.

Delivering the four Es will make it hard for clients to leave you because of their emotional connection and the way they are treated. When you engage with prospects in the same way, they will also be drawn to you.

To assist you as you read, consider what you are doing now and what needs to change. What can you and/or your team do to elevate the client and prospect experience and relate more effectively with every individual? Consider also how much more business you will acquire by improving the experience people have.

The experience and relationship they want with you is very clear:

- *They don't want to be taken for granted.*
- *They don't want to be referred to as "an account" or as part of your "client or customer base."*
- *They want to be treated as individuals.*
- *They want to be remembered.*
- *They want personalized and humanized communications.*
- *They want an elevated experience, not just "expected good service."*

- *They want to feel significant to you.*

- *They want an emotional connection.*

- *They want economic security.*

- *They want proactive, understandable, meaningful communications.*

- *They want to build a portfolio of great memories about their experience with you, your team, and your company.*

I will address each of these needs and many more in detail with a specific tactic to ensure you are meeting each one. In Chapter 8, I will provide several action steps you can use to implement these tactics into your business.

As you read, be mindful that, after all is said and done:

RELATIONSHIPS DRIVE REVENUE. BUILD THEM AND YOU WILL THRIVE.

Or, as my good friend and fellow Hall of Fame speaker Patricia Fripp says so well, *"Don't celebrate closing a sale, celebrate opening a relationship."*

CHAPTER 2

HOW TO PERSONALIZE COMMUNICATIONS AND SHOW CLIENTS AND PROSPECTS YOU CARE

All the available technology, as useful as it is to process business, contact people, and track interactions, *cannot* take the place of you and the relationship you build with your clients and prospective clients.

People want to be psychologically reassured they are in the right place.

While many organizations and professionals promote and speak about their client-/customer-centric culture, they focus on the strategic "what" versus the tactical "how."

Written communications, such as notes, emails, and even texts, are often without relational tone and lack the graciousness and sense of connection and belonging that people seek.

This also occurs in some verbal communications. Given the pressure of the day-to-day, it is not hard to sometimes be short with people, be less than gracious, and just be very matter of fact and in some cases terse. You may not "mean to," but clients still deserve better. They are the only reason you have the business you have.

You cannot let your bad day become their bad day.

Even social media posts often lack personal relevance and a relational tone. They may be well-written and tout how great your organization is and how wonderfully you are doing, but consider how much more effective, relational, and elevated your posts would be if your client's personal stories were central to the posting—their stories about how the experience they have with you makes all the difference.

Ask your client if you can share a personal or professional success they have had, and they will be thrilled that you are interested in them and care about them—regardless of whether they allow you to post it to social media.

Personalization and humanization are vital components of a caring, thoughtful, client-centric culture today. People want personalization and humanization, with no exceptions.

Consumers define personalization as *tailoring all interactions, touchpoints, and communications to me and who I am as an individual. I do not want to be just a number or an account.*

They define humanization as *treating me in a respectful, civilized manner and communicating with me in an understandable way that I relate to and appreciate.*

With this understanding, take advantage of every interaction with a client and prospect to make it meaningful by personalizing and humanizing it. Whether it is face-to-face, by email or phone, or in social media posts, this approach reassures them that you see them not just as an account but as an individual.

The more personalized their interaction with you is, the better their experience will be. The better the experience, the deeper their relationship and emotional bond with you and your company will be.

Personalization helps them feel confident they are in the right place and with the right professional. It gives them faith that you will deliver exactly what they want. Ultimately, it helps transform them into delighted advocates.

Against this backdrop, consider these words of wisdom.

"BE MINDFUL WHEN IT COMES TO YOUR WORDS. A STRING OF SOME THAT DON'T MEAN MUCH TO YOU, MAY STICK WITH SOMEONE ELSE FOR A LIFETIME."

—RACHEL WOLCHIN

"BE CAREFUL WITH YOUR WORDS. ONCE THEY ARE SAID, THEY CAN BE ONLY FORGIVEN, NOT FORGOTTEN."

—UNKNOWN

As illustrated by these timeless quotes, the words we write and say have a profound impact on people's perception of you and your organization. People want to have meaningful exchanges and conversations with you and be treated as individuals.

When you personalize and humanize your communications, you demonstrate that you truly care about them.

In a world where personal communications have been reduced to abbreviations like "lol," "ttyl," and "lmk," personalization and humanization are often lost.

Clients want their professional, regardless of industry or product, to give them crisp, clear, relationally styled messages both verbally and in writing that clearly express "you are important to me."

The following tactics will give you guidance and clarity on how to personalize and humanize every interaction by talking and writing to clients and prospective clients as individuals. This way, your clients will know that you care about them and that the word "client-centric" is not just a word but their experienced reality.

Remember:

"WORDS ARE FREE. IT'S HOW YOU USE THEM THAT MAY COST YOU."

—REV. J. MARTIN

TACTIC 1: THE POWER OF A NAME

I use my middle name, Richard, instead of my first name, Charles, because my dad was Charles. However, I do use my first initial formally, as C. Richard. You can only imagine how many emails I get that begin *Dear C.* Those don't get read, since I know that they don't know or care to know enough about me to call me Richard.

With the technology that exists today, there is no reason for anyone to receive a communication that addresses them as anything but their preferred name.

There is no reason whatsoever for "Dear client or dear policyholder or dear anything" except the preferred name of the client.

The most important thing to people is and always has been:

Their name! Specifically, the name they like to be addressed by, whether that is their given name or a nickname.

It matters more than you might imagine. Always ask for and *use* prospects' and clients' preferred name.

David may like Dave.
Samuel may like Samuel.
Dr. Donna Wilson likely wants to be addressed as Dr. Wilson.
Elizabeth may like Beth or Liz—find out which!
Remember, T. Boone Pickens never went by T.

TACTIC 2: I BET YOU CAN SPELL YOUR NAME

How often have you been asked *"Can you spell your name?"*

Not only is it somewhat nonsensical to ask that, but it also demonstrates the lack of awareness of the person doing the asking.

Of course you can spell your name, and so can your client.

I was reminded again of this last evening checking in to a hotel at ten thirty with a bag in tow and only me and the front desk clerk in the lobby. The first question I was asked was *"Checking in?"* Yes. Then I was asked, *"Can you spell your name?"*

This inane question needs to be replaced with a more gracious one: *"Please spell your name so that I can capture it correctly."*

Then, unless their name is Nelson or Smith or Jones, I always ask them to pronounce their first and last name. You would be amazed how many thank me for making sure I can pronounce it correctly.

And FYI, I do the same on my written introduction when I am going to be presenting so people can say my last name correctly. I spell it out phonetically—Weylman is pronounced "while-men"—and I get so many thank yous for that phonetic spelling by the person introducing me.

TACTIC 3: NO PROBLEM, NO WORRIES = NO VALUE

When a client makes a request and says, *"thank you"* when it is handled, the unfortunate common response is *"no problem"* or *"no worries."* I said *"no problem"* plenty until I had a client say, *"What do you mean no problem? I didn't think it was a problem to ask you a question—after all, I am your client. If it is a problem, just let me know."* Ouch! So glad she told me!

It is far better to say, *"my pleasure"* or *"happy to help."* These responses have even more relational value than the traditional *"you're welcome."*

"My pleasure" and *"happy to help"* reinforce your value, your relationship with them, and their importance to you. It also encourages additional questions and requests, which adds tremendous value to the relationship and allows you to get to know them better.

TACTIC 4: COMMUNICATE MORE GRACIOUSLY AND AT A HIGHER LEVEL

Along the same line as the previous tactic, *all* words matter.

Think about the impression you have when you order a steak at a restaurant. Which is better to hear: *"How do you want it cooked?"* or *"How do you enjoy it?"*

Or as you're eating your meal, which is better to hear: *"Still working on it?"* or *"Are you still enjoying?"*

When someone calls in do you sometimes ask them to *"Hang on a second?"*

Wouldn't it be better to say, *"May I place you on hold?"* and wait for a response?

Are *please* and *thank you* part of your lexicon?

Ask yourself, am I communicating at a higher level and graciously with the people I interact with daily? Do people feel uplifted after they communicate with me?

Chick-fil-A has built a fast-food empire, and yet rarely do people mention their good chicken. Instead, people mention the politeness of the staff's words. Elevated words say *I am communicating with you as a person and not just at you as a transaction.*

TACTIC 5: WALMART UNDERSTANDS HOW TO OFFER HELP

Often the first thing we hear when we enter a place of business or call an office to reach someone is *"Can I help you?"* And often in understaffed organizations or during busy times, this question is spit out with no inflection. Unfortunately, it comes across as terse, and with the wrong inflection it can sound like you are annoyed.

"How may I help you?" is far more gracious and personal.

Even Walmart realized the issue with *"Can I help you?"* They took that phrase off their employee's aprons and replaced it with *"How may I help you?"*

TACTIC 6: DO I NEED YOUR PERMISSION TO CALL?

How you encourage clients to contact you is another area where you can elevate the client's experience and demonstrate that you value their business and relationship.

The modus operandi for most people is to sign off verbally or in a written piece with *"Feel free to give me a call."*

This might seem nice, but they don't need your permission to call. It is far better to say, *"Feel welcome to call."*

Once when I was speaking at a conference in New York, a top financial advisor who had heard me speak previously on how to elevate the client experience to stand apart from the competition was in attendance, joined by his two daughters who were in business with him. I had mentioned this tactic at the previous meeting, and he had implemented it into his business. Giving further evidence of the power of this personalized, humanized tweak, when I mentioned this tactic in response to a question his daughters spoke up. They said, *"Several of our clients mentioned how much they liked the warmer, more gracious words."*

Clearly, *"Feel welcome to call"* sets you apart as more gracious, caring, kind, and thoughtful than others. Plus, it silently says to the client, "I value you, and I am here for you."

TACTIC 7: SIGN YOUR EMAILS AND ALL OTHER CORRESPONDENCE RELATIONALLY

Several years ago, I noticed a trend with email signatures increasingly closing with signoffs like "Best" and "Sincerely yours."

Curious about this, our consulting team asked people we interviewed as part of rebranding projects done for various firms what they thought of these signatures.

The client perception was crystal clear that "Best" is not relational at all. In fact, some said, "What do they mean by Best? Best what? Best for them or what?" And the institutional "Sincerely yours" is perceived as neither relational nor sincere.

So, avoid closing your emails or other correspondence with signoffs like these.

Instead, use a more personal, less institutional phrase, such as "Warm regards" or "Best regards."

TACTIC 8: BE SURE YOUR TELEPHONE MAKES A GREAT FIRST IMPRESSION

We all understand the cost savings of automated phone systems. However, the frustration we all have with overly complicated automated systems diminishes the client's experience of reaching you and your team.

The way your phone is answered and navigated matters. For automated systems, be sure the greeting is warm, and the navigation is easy. Have you ever called *your* number and worked through the menu to determine if the messaging is clear and welcoming, and the navigation is easy?

If you have an actual person answering the telephone, it is important to realize that the impression this person gives can also make or break your client's loyalty. People calling in on a land line expect to be greeted pleasantly and professionally.

We all can remember times, however, when that has not been the case. When reading online reviews of people's experiences with companies, it is very telling how many people comment on the way the telephone was answered. *Rude, on hold forever, sent me to voicemail, said "hold, please" and then dumped my call.*

When people read these reviews, it influences their decision on whether to engage. Even worse, if this happens to them as a client, it seriously erodes any perception that you deliver an elevated experience. For this reason, you should have a warm, gracious, and friendly standard script that everyone who answers the telephone follows.

Example: *Hi, thank you for calling Richard Weylman's office. This is Selina. How may I help you?*

Some companies elevate their receptionist position by naming that person the Director of First Impressions. Whether you have a person answering the phone or an automated system, that is the truth.

TACTIC 9: BE INTERRUPTIBLE AND NOT AN INTERRUPTER

Your day is full, so time is important. Consequently, it is easy to get impatient and interrupt clients to get them to ask their question or explain their point more quickly.

One word to be mindful of here is *patience*. When people feel that they can express themselves openly and that you are actually interested and listening, they reveal many things that interrupters never hear or uncover. Conversely if a client interrupts you with questions or comments, that is a clear sign that they are interested and are relying on you. So, be interruptible, not the interrupter.

TACTIC 10: WHAT TO DO WHEN SOMEONE ELSE INTERRUPTS YOU AND A CLIENT

What should you say when you are on a call with a client or engaged in a discussion in person and someone calls on your other line? Don't say *"Hang on a second"* or, as I was told recently, *"Let me get rid of this other call."* How would the client like to be the call that you were "getting rid of"? Instead, simply say, *"Excuse me a moment, may I place you on a brief hold?"* and wait for an answer. How many times have you experienced someone answering the phone and mid-sentence they stop you with *"hold on"* and place you on hold without waiting for your acknowledgment? How does that make you feel?

TACTIC 11: ARE YOU UNAVAILABLE OR ARE YOU JUST DODGING MY CALL?

I was walking through a real estate office recently and heard an assistant tell an incoming caller, *"Let me see if he wants to take your call right now."* Yikes! The broker was sitting right there in his office reading what looked like a newspaper.

If that assistant goes back to that caller and says he is unavailable, what is the subliminal message the caller receives? *He doesn't want to talk with me right now. I guess I am not that important.*

The words you use matter to the hearer. So, when someone asks for someone who is in the office but may not be available, simply say, *"Let me see if he/she is available or on another call."*

TACTIC 12: SET A TELEPHONE APPOINTMENT TO AVOID SENDING PEOPLE TO VOICEMAIL

When someone calls in to an office and the person they ask for is not in or is in a meeting, the common response is, *"Would you like their voicemail?"* Avoid this and instead thoughtfully and graciously offer to assist them:

"They're not in the office—how may I help you?"

If you cannot help them, offer to set a telephone appointment for them to receive a call from the person they asked for instead of sending them to voicemail. Here is an example:

> *I understand. He/she is [at an educational meeting, conducting research, meeting with a client such as yourself, on another call (not line), etc.]. However, he/she is available later today between two and four o'clock. Let's set a telephone appointment during that time—what time works best for you?*

This simple, thoughtful, caring approach not only elevates the caller's experience but also reinforces once again that they are important. It also subliminally tells them they are respected and that you are there for them.

A key point for implementation is that everyone in the office should have access to each other's calendar. Being client-centric requires it.

TACTIC 13: BE GRACIOUS AND POSITIVE WHEN YOU ARE LATE IN REPLYING OR ATTENDING

Every time I see an email that says, *"I am sorry for taking so long to reply"* or someone joins a call or meeting late and says, *"I am sorry,"* it disappoints me. Why? I am disappointed that people don't realize how self-deprecating that statement is about themselves. It also injects negativity into communications. When you are late getting an email out, instead of starting on a negative note, simply say, *"Thank you for your patience with this reply."* If you are late to a virtual or in-person meeting/luncheon/dinner, replace that negative *"I am sorry"* messaging with *"My apologies."*

TACTIC 14: GET TURNED ON TO THESE TRENDY WORDS AND PHRASES THAT NEED CLARIFICATION

There is always a torrent of trendy words and phrases that people let slip into their vocabulary. The problem is not that they are bad but that they become so overused that they lose their power and ability to provide clarity. Or, worse, they are misinterpreted because not everyone uses or understands them. Though they refer to specific things and concepts that are sometimes relevant to a discussion, take the time to clarify exactly what you mean. Not everyone understands what you mean by stakeholders, or supply chain issues, or impactful, or crowdsourcing. The smallest tweaks in the words you use have a profound impact on the outcome and perception by the receiver. Here are some trendy words that, as of this writing, often need clarification for the reader or listener:

Our policy	Circle back	Crowdsourcing
World-class	Side hustle	Stakeholders
Humbled	Press/lean in	Misinformation
Pivot	Impactful	Mandate
Metrics	Toxic	Protocols
New normal	Literally	Ecosystem
It is what it is	To be honest	In these uncertain times
Supply chain issues	Robust	Out of an abundance of caution
Unprecedented	Leverage	
Voice your concerns	Synergy	Authentic

And be mindful of new trendy words you let slip into your communications going forward so that you specifically clarify what you mean.

TACTIC 15: USE LIVELY WORDS TO ENERGIZE AND CLARIFY YOUR COMMUNICATIONS

Use words such as these:

Prepare	Play	Pinpoint
Increase	Demonstrate	Focus
Identify	Explore	Divide
Define	Draft	Avoid
Create	Use	Set
Interface	Describe	Change
Develop	Determine	Improve
List	Train	Monitor
Distinguish	Select	Transfer
Perform	Make	Get
Match	Master	Find
Design	Write	Sketch
Structure	Overcome	Apply
Foster	Handle	Organize
Build	See	Examine
Conduct	View	

TACTIC 16: BE MINDFUL OF YOUR WRITTEN AND VERBAL TONE

A financial advisor wrote to me and wanted to know why, after writing to one of his best clients, they *"were upset with his tone."* What was the tone?

His email to them after their meeting stated, *"We will **ultimately** honor the decision you make, **but I strongly encourage you to…**"* and then rehashed all the points made when they had met in person.

Words and phrases like *"ultimately"* and *"but I strongly encourage you to"* do not instill confidence or a sense that you care.

Your clients will have different opinions and, as you know, will not always accept your recommendations or solutions. However, you will damage your client relationship if they sense you are annoyed or are pushing them in a direction they don't want to go at this time.

When you differ in opinion, be gracious and communicate in a positive tone. His email to them after their meeting could have said:

> *We understand your position and appreciate you sharing it with us. We will move forward as you have asked. However, we have identified a few other points we did not discuss that you may wish to consider before we take the next steps with your request. When can we have a short call to share this additional information? Please advise and thank you.*

TACTIC 17: BE SURE TO REFERENCE THEIR DESIRED OUTCOME, NOT THEIR ACCOUNT

Nobody wants to be merely an account. What they want is to achieve their goals.

If you are an air conditioning technician scheduler, clients want their air conditioning working correctly, not for you to check to see their account. It is better to check their previous service record.

If you're an attorney, what they want is for you to reference and review the progress on their claim, case, action, or plea, not their account. If you are a doctor, would you say, *"Let me look at your account,"* or would you say, *"Let me look at your medical records and test results to see where you are and what we can do"*?

If you're in the insurance business, don't review my account; please *review my coverage*. If you are in the car repair business, please *review my repair order*, not my account. If you are a financial professional, please *review my financial objectives* or *my plan*, not my account.

And be mindful that clients have been taught by you and others to ask about their accounts.

Change that today so they see the actual value you are delivering on their behalf by referencing their desired outcome. When they say, *"I want to check my account,"* reset and tell them, *"I would be happy to check the progress on your plan"* or *"your level of coverage"* or *"progress we are making on your repairs."* Elevate your relationship by talking about the outcome you provide so they never forget why they are doing business with you.

TACTIC 18: PAY ATTENTION TO THE LITTLE THINGS

We all know, or should know, that relationships drive revenue. The root of relationships, of course, is the ability to focus on people and relate to and with them. There are innumerable ways to accomplish this, and you will discover many throughout this book. However, to help you begin to focus on and pay attention to the little things, here are a few examples that make a difference.

Ask people where they went to school and note that in their client record. Inquiring about or referencing their alma mater sports teams enables you to discover much more about them and relate with them.

I had a prospect who went to a school where spectators at sporting events did a hand gesture called "the Claw" to encourage their players on the field. Imagine his reaction when I told him I was curious and had heard about this hand gesture and asked him about doing "the Claw." Our relationship went to a whole new and deeper level.

Of course, you also want to get your clients' children's and grandchildren's names and inquire about them from time to time. However, always mention their actual names instead of just saying *"I hope the kids/grandkids are doing well."*

And don't forget pets. People who have pets appreciate those who ask about or do something thoughtful for them.

As an example, a young financial advisor had an elderly couple come aboard as new clients. They were to come in and sign some final transfer papers but cancelled at the last minute because their dog had a leg injury.

The advisor did what any good advisor would do: she offered to come to their house to get the paperwork done for them.

But she did one more thing that others would likely not do—something that set her apart and demonstrated her kindness, empathy, thoughtfulness, and caring.

She asked, *"What type of dog do you have, and what is the dog's name?"*

She then stopped at Petco and bought a tin of dog biscuits and a get-well card for their dog and took those to the clients' home.

They are now clients for life. Moreover, their son, who is a neurosurgeon, was so impressed by her thoughtfulness and empathy that he and his four partners in another state moved all their business to her.

A young man who works in a car dealership in Seattle has similar results when he thoughtfully and proactively gives a personally branded umbrella to all his clients for those wet Seattle days.

And a receptionist in California notes the favorite beverage of every client with an appointment in the coming week and ensures it is available.

Thoughtfulness, empathy, caring, and kindness are valuable relationship-building traits that no amount of competitor marketing dollars can defeat. And of course, given the law of reciprocity, the little things almost always lead to bigger things.

TACTIC 19: IF YOU'RE OUT OF THE OFFICE, BE SURE YOU DON'T SHUT THEM OUT

Everyone deserves a break, and if you're out of the office for a day or longer, it is customary to have an automated out-of-office email and/or voice message. However, I am amazed by some of the out-of-office messages I have seen.

Here are a handful I have recently received that really leave their clients hanging:

> *Sorry, I am out of the office for the next two weeks and will not be checking messages.*

> *I am out of the office and have limited internet service and will not be able to respond quickly if at all. Sorry.*

> *I am out of the office until June 6 (received on June 30).*

Maybe the worst: *Due to my workload I will likely not be able to reply to you for ten days.*

When you are unable to respond to an email or call, use a more gracious message such as *"Thank you for your email (or call). The good news is, although I am out of the office, my assistant or partner (name) will be delighted to help you. Feel welcome to call xxx-xxx-xxxx."*

TACTIC 20: CLOSE THE LOOP AND FILL THEM WITH GRATITUDE

When a client makes a request, or when they are aware you will do or are doing something on their behalf, avoid leaving them in the dark. Give them progress reports, even if the request is a simple one.

In all cases, close the loop and let them know *"I have taken care of it on your behalf."* Proactively communicating progress and completion builds value and increases their sense that you care about them.

A friend of mine started a sign and printing business in southwest Florida. He has built a substantial business by getting people to move their printing and sign business to him.

When he asked why they left his competitor and joined him, they repeatedly stated, *"It was just too difficult to get status updates on our jobs. Our hope is you will do better."* Now, he gives proactive job updates to all of his clients, and he always gets a positive reply. Even if it is just "Got it," that is enough to close the loop!

Here is another example of closing the loop that everyone appreciates and that will drive clients' business and their advocacy.

One member of my team has a nephew who is in the business of building docks, and his business is exploding. We asked him how he was experiencing so much growth and success in a very regulated business. He said, *"I answer the phone, and I call people back who leave a message. My competitors don't."*

Oh, the joy of thoughtful communications.

TACTIC 21: POSITIVITY BUILDS AND ATTRACTS

Many people today are living and working in stressful circumstances. They are caught in a vicious cycle of trying to do enough to have enough to be enough. Thus, people are drawn to and grateful for positive messages and interactions. My friend and bestselling author Shep Hyken says, *"The word 'no' is not in our vocabulary. We use positive words when answering customers."*

Case in point: A client recently asked a question of an entrepreneur who makes custom promotional products. The client wanted to know if they could get three specific pieces branded with their logo and color. He started his response with *"Yes,"* and then explained the minimums and the set-up fees. What the client hears is the yes.

Contrast that with the waiter at a restaurant where I was having lunch recently. He asked how I wanted my hamburger cooked. I asked for it rare and the waiter responded, *"No, but we will make it medium rare."* If rare wasn't an option, I should have been told and explained why. When my colleague heard his response, she was ready to stand up and leave.

No matter what circumstances you find yourself in, it is essential that you are a positive influence on your clients. Positivity builds and attracts; negativity destroys and repels. Focus on your gratefulness for their business and not on your circumstances. Yes, the phone is ringing off the hook, people are impatient, and you have issues at home to deal with. While these circumstances may be difficult, your client does not need to feel their effects.

Research shows that well over two thirds of people say that when people they interact with show a positive, can-do attitude, it keeps them engaged and calm in stressful situations. They feel cared about and cared for, which is gold in this world that many describe as self-centered.

Consequently, in communication, whether in person, by telephone, or online, people consider not only what is said but also what they observe. That said, always be friendly, interested, and focused on them.

I knew Truett Cathy, the late founder of Chick-fil-A, and he said, *"We aren't really in the chicken business, we are in the people business."* Ultimately, we are all in the people business too.

CHAPTER 3

HOW TO MAKE CLIENTS AND PROSPECTS FEEL SECURE EMOTIONALLY

Security is a driving force in life, and it is also important in choosing with whom we do business. Tomes have been written and millions spent on teaching sales professionals ways they can be more confident so that people will buy from them. While such training is certainly important, what is often overlooked is that the client and prospect *also* needs to feel confident and secure, both emotionally and economically, about their decisions.

Economically, there are many factors they consider. Central to economic security is that they want to feel confident they are getting a fair price and a clear outcome that suits their objectives, needs, and desires. Simply put, they ultimately want to get what they want and paid for.

It used to be the case that if you were the low-price provider, that was enough to capture business. However, today, no matter the type of business you are in, emotion also plays a central role in nearly every purchase decision and relationship you have with a client or prospective client.

In this age of innumerable choices, people want to feel they are talking with the right person, the right company, and that they are doing the right thing. In the next two chapters, I will provide you with prescriptive tactics to make clients and prospects feel secure both emotionally and economically.

LET'S BEGIN WITH EMOTIONAL SECURITY

When people feel emotionally insecure, as they often do, they lack the confidence to engage. If they are already clients and things occur that reduce their emotional security, they might begin to wonder: *Should I stay with you?*

When you focus on clients and prospects personally and elevate their experience by doing things that build their emotional security, they become comfortable. They feel as though you know and understand them and are empathetic to their situation and desires. They see you as someone they can confide in about issues you can help them solve. This sense of emotional security creates many opportunities for them, and they will be open to doing more and more business with you. If you build up their emotional security, they will not go anywhere.

Thus, the emotional component of their security is very important and needs to be reinforced by the actions you take each time you engage on their behalf. It is not to be ignored!

TACTIC 22: POSITION YOUR WORK BASED ON SOLUTIONS, NOT ON PRICING

Everything you buy has a price. People expect that, and they find it odd that many businesses tend to lead with their price. For example, Walmart used to lead with "*Low Prices Every Day*," until they realized that "*Save Money. Live Better.*" was a far better description of what they provide consumers. This type of solution-based positioning has paid off big.

Unfortunately, many professionals and companies still position and describe their business based on how or what they charge or how they get paid (commission-based or fee-based). *Ugh!*

Physicians don't run a fee-based or commission-based practice. They run a curative practice. They are paid for the counsel and solutions they provide.

Successful people in the trades, like plumbers, handymen, remodelers, roofers, and carpet cleaning service professionals, don't initially talk about what or how they charge when describing their business. Instead, they talk about what they deliver: open drains, refreshed rooms, roofs that don't leak, clean carpets, and odor removal.

So, with that understanding, why would you describe your business based on how you get paid as a fee-based or a commission-based business?

Instead, let people know you run an advice- or outcome-based business. Examples might include, *I help people find the home of their dreams, I help people sort out their life choices, I help people get their financial life in balance, I help people plan and achieve the retirement they deserve, or I run a restaurant where people get to hang out and have fun.* You get the idea.

When you describe your business based on how you get paid or what you charge the client, they will focus on only one thing: how much? As I discussed in detail in my last book, *The Power of Why: Breaking Out in a Competitive Marketplace*, the quickest way to erode trust and confidence is to encourage people to focus on your cost versus your value.

TACTIC 23: WHAT TO SAY WHEN ASKED SOCIALLY, "WHAT DO YOU DO?"

As a professional, when someone asks, *"What do you do?"* you have a great opportunity to build a solid emotional connection and set the table for their economic security. The key is to not focus solely on your role description (e.g., I am a medical professional, real estate agent, attorney, financial advisor, general manager of a restaurant, butcher, baker, or candlestick maker).

Instead of talking about you, talk about the outcome you deliver for people like them. This approach immediately sets you apart by creating curiosity. Do not do what most people do, which is to focus on themselves and try to convince people to engage. Your answer should be about the outcome you can deliver, not about you and your expertise. Here are a couple of examples.

I enjoy what I do as a real estate agent because my mission is helping my clients find their dream home in the location they desire. My focus is on their stage of life and their desired lifestyle.

I enjoy what I do as a financial professional because my mission is to help my clients find comprehensive solutions to enjoy a sound financial future. My focus is on their stage of life, and their future retirement needs.

In all cases, a critical step is to *stop talking* after this initial introduction. Your objective in a social setting should be to build a connection between you and the other person—not to sell to them, but rather to demonstrate that you are not all about yourself.

This approach shows that you are thoughtful and empathetic. You illustrate through your words that you can speak their language by identifying the outcome they may be seeking.

When you stop talking, the big payoff for you is that they will be curious and may ask, "How do you do that?" This creates an opportunity to meet after the social event. To make that happen, here is how you should answer:

I would be happy to let you know how I am able to do that. Let's have breakfast or lunch next week, and after we have a conversation about what and how I do things, I would love to hear more about what you do as well. How about next...

Here, you are positioning yourself as a true professional who is sensitive to building their emotional security and a relationship.

Another ancillary and important benefit is when you stop talking the other person will begin talking and asking questions. When you get them talking, you will learn ways to personalize and humanize future communications with them.

TACTIC 24: BE SURE YOUR ONLINE PRESENCE IS ABOUT WHAT YOU DO FOR PEOPLE

Every generation is looking for someone who not only has expertise but "understands" them and what they are looking for. To discover this, today's buyers will go online to check you and perhaps your company out first before they even consider engaging.

Most websites and professional social media profiles are all about the company or the professional—in other words, you, and your credentials. While this may be something you are proud of, that doesn't matter.

What matters is that your website, your social profile, starts with what you help people accomplish!

That is what they are looking for, so state it clearly. This helps them sense that you understand them before they even engage with you. Once you state what they can accomplish through you (save money and retire better, get a jumbo mortgage, safeguard their financial future, manage complex estate matters, keep their equipment running, etc.), then tell them something about your outside interests and then your credentials. Create a sense of emotional engagement and security immediately by illustrating that you are there for them.

Be sure your photographs are recent and that all your social sites are consistent. Avoid inconsistency across multiple social sites so that clients and potential clients are not confused.

TACTIC 25: RESUSCITATE AND ELEVATE YOUR LOBBY

I was very surprised to visit a financial office several years ago and see on its lobby coffee table a magazine with a cover article titled *How to Be Sure You Have the Right Advisor*. Interesting reading, I am sure, for a waiting client or prospect—who might begin to wonder about you based on that article. *Yikes!*

If you are going to have reading materials, be sure they are aspirational and not gloom and doom news rags. The same goes for pictures on the lobby walls. Make them aspirational so people can see themselves in them as part of their dream and/or desired outcome.

Be aware that the surroundings you immerse a client in reflect who you are and how you see them. Avoid focusing on how good you are and focus instead on how what you offer will be good for them.

Place your value promise prominently on your lobby wall to subtly remind clients of what you are accomplishing for them. Isn't that what all successful retailers do as they market themselves through their stores and online platforms?

Have coffee and tea available with a selection of brews. One of our clients who serves families with small children set up a play area in a corner of the lobby. This keeps the child occupied and the client less stressed. For those clients without children in tow, this thoughtful accommodation still makes a positive impression since it shows that these professionals and this firm care about people.

TACTIC 26: ELEVATE YOUR WORK AND CONFERENCE SPACE

Recently, I was doing an office experience audit for a firm in the southwestern US. They wanted to know not only how to better elevate their clients' experience but what else they could do to make people feel "more comfortable."

One young lady there really had it right, and her office became the model for others to consider for their offices.

Her office and conference room were decorated in colors of the Latino community she served, and she had a collage on the wall of pictures of all her clients' children and grandchildren, with a note underneath to clients: *Don't forget to bring your latest pictures so we can see whose future we are safeguarding.* Brilliant.

The key overall strategy here is that your workspace should reflect your values.

So, while you may value sales awards, as others in this office did, it is still best to remove them. Awards that say "I am the highest, the best, the top gross sales leader, etc." can give people the impression you are all about yourself. Display instead your credentials, your accreditations, and kind notes from clients. Take all your award plaques and trophies and keep them in your private home office.

Along the same lines, don't be afraid to share personal things that are important to you (e.g., family photos, charity work photos, etc.), but be careful not to brag about things you do for others. As you build trust and an emotional connection, clients feel privileged being let into your "inner circle," which increases the trust factor on both sides.

For your conference space, have a checklist to be sure that where you have conversations gives clients a sense of security and comfort.

Consider these suggestions as a starting point. You will discover more as you read on.

- *Clean off the last meeting's whiteboards and clean up meeting areas.*

- *Have the Wi-Fi password printed out so clients can log in easily if needed.*

- *Have pads of paper and pens on the meeting table for clients. This encourages them to take notes and subliminally suggests that the information being presented is important.*

- *Pretest any video being used.*

- *Have wipes and tissues available on the conference table.*

- *Have a spare company-branded umbrella available in case it starts to rain when clients are ready to leave.*

TACTIC 27: WHEN YOU MEET PEOPLE, BE SURE YOU ARE GRACIOUS AND WELCOMING

Too often, the first time we meet someone, we say, *"Hi, nice to meet you,"* and they awkwardly say, *"Nice to meet you too."* No relational tone or true connection.

Or if we know them, we just say, *"Hi, how are you?"* It is the default greeting for most of us. However, that typically results in a perfunctory *"Fine, thanks."*

Neither greeting is gracious or very welcoming. A far more considerate approach when you meet someone for the first time *or* greet someone you know and have met before is to say, *"Hi, nice to see you."*

There are two key reasons why it is important to say "see" versus "meet" in these situations, even if you have never met before.

First, it is possible that you *have* met them before and forgotten. We have all had that embarrassing experience, and it is best avoided!

Second, it immediately engages people and puts them at ease. They will often say, with a bit of a raised octave, *"Oh, nice to see you too."*

I mentioned this approach at an entrepreneurial conference in New York a few years ago in response to a question on the best way to greet people. The young lady who asked the question emailed me a couple of months later and said her future mother-in law thought she was *"so thoughtful"* because she *"always made people feel welcomed by saying 'nice to see you.' "* Talk about an unexpected consequence! However, if you have in-laws, take note.

News flash: As I am writing this, I just received a text from a colleague sharing the new Breeze Airlines app. When you open it, what comes up is a message that says, *"It's nice to see you."*

TACTIC 28: DON'T JUST SAY YOU EMPATHIZE—DEMONSTRATE EMPATHY

In today's business environment, people are seeking professionals who demonstrate that they have empathy for them instead of just saying *"I understand,"* or *"I empathize with you."* Many people perceive these words as a generic *"sorry about that, but let's move on."*

When it comes to asking sensitive questions—whether business or personal—it is essential to be mindful that many people are emotional about the answers.

You build real emotional currency when you say *"if you don't mind me asking"* at the *end* of the question to demonstrate empathy. Saying it at the beginning *always* puts people on guard as they think *"oh, now what?"* or *"okay, here it comes."*

Here are some examples of empathetically asking personal questions:

- *How is your family member (name, relationship) recovering…if you don't mind me asking?*

- *You mentioned your son/daughter (name) was struggling with school. How is he/she doing now…if you don't mind me asking?*

Example of empathetic business questions:

- *Who is your current financial advisor…if you don't mind me asking?*

- *How much are you considering investing in your dream home…if you don't mind me asking?*

- *What are your total savings and investments to date…if you don't mind me asking?*

- *What types of family issues do you want to address…if you don't mind me asking?*

- *What is your plan if the house doesn't sell in six months...if you don't mind me asking?*

- *What's holding you back...if you don't mind me asking?*

Empathy creates emotional security and thus a deep sense that you are thoughtful, kind, and caring. When you demonstrate empathy, the emotional currency you will gain with the client is bankable.

TACTIC 29: USE EYE CONTACT TO AVOID BEING SEEN AS SOMEONE WITH "I" TROUBLE

We have all experienced it—we are trying to converse with someone, and they are looking over our shoulder to see who else or what else they should be focused on. We see this as annoying and disrespectful behavior by a self-centered individual. Don't fall into that trap. I have been an interview guest on dozens of TV shows, radio shows, and podcasts, and I have consistently found that the best hosts are the ones who make you feel like there is no one else with whom they would like to be talking.

Remember that when a client or prospective client is speaking with you, you are the host. Be the host that makes eye contact and reinforces to them that there is no one else you would rather be talking to than them. This will make them feel cared for and emotionally secure that finally there is someone who wants to hear what is important to them.

Also, when you are meeting with anyone, put that cell phone away. Along with avoiding eye contact, constantly looking at messages, even with the volume off, tells the client that he or she is less important than the phone. If you are expecting a call from a child or a loved one who is sick, explain the situation to the client and ask their permission or thank them for their patience.

TACTIC 30: SERVE THAT BEVERAGE ELEGANTLY

I recommended in a previous tactic to have coffee and tea available for your clients. To take that experience to another level, offer a menu of two or three teas and coffees, as luxury retailers often do.

Serve chilled water in a pitcher and provide fine glasses.

Skip the Styrofoam. (And remember, if it looks like Styrofoam, it is Styrofoam.) Instead, serve the coffee or tea in a china cup. If you choose to serve a beverage in a custom mug from your firm, offer it as a gift and have it rinsed out and placed in a box afterward for the client.

Premium coffee shops like Starbucks have spent a small fortune to create a recyclable cup that feels like china on the lip. The same attention to detail not only elevates the experience but also says to people, *"You are special."* People who feel special do business because they feel they are in the right place.

I had a gentleman in Montana implement this tactic with his rancher clients. He now serves their coffee in china cups when they are in the office. He said that even though his client's thumbs were too big to fit through the little handles on the cups, they kept telling him that *"he is the most sophisticated professional in Montana"* and that *"they feel special"* because of the way he treats them. This is certainly a very good ROI on a set of four china cups and saucers from the thrift store.

TACTIC 31: HELP THEM GET RECHARGED WHEN THEY ARE IN YOUR OFFICE

People rely on their devices for communication. There is very little that frustrates people more than their phones or other devices they carry running on empty. How many times have you had a conversation end because *"My phone is dying"*? When people are visiting your office, provide a basket of charging cables for every common device and phone. While they are conferring with you, proactively offer, *"If you would like to charge your phone while we have our conversation, I have charging cables."*

I love the Uber and Lyft drivers that offer a phone charging cable proactively. While it only happens occasionally, when it does, a five-star rating and a much bigger tip are their rewards for being thoughtful, kind, and caring.

TACTIC 32: WALK THEM TO OTHER AREAS THEY NEED TO VISIT

If someone needs to use the restroom or make a private phone call from an empty room, walk them to that location. It is not enough to point and say, *"It is down the hall on the right, you can't miss it"* (until of course they do). Take the cue from some big box stores and Whole Foods. They don't tell you where to go to find what you want; most of the time, they take you there.

TACTIC 33: BE SURE TO CONSIDER YOUR RESTROOMS

Whether your restrooms are private to your place of business or down the common hall on your floor, the restrooms should have tissues replenished daily. Plus, be sure there are wipes on the counter, not just paper towels in a dispenser. We have all been subjected to nasty, and nasty isn't elevated. Be mindful that even if your restroom is in a common use hallway, a small sign that reads *"tissues and wipes courtesy of…"* says that here is a company, a team, an individual who is thoughtful, kind, and caring.

TACTIC 34: BE SURE THEY HAVE A PRIVATE PLACE TO DISCUSS THEIR ISSUES

I was in a bank recently where a loan officer had the door to his office open and loudly asked the couple in front of him, "*So, you want a loan of $18,000 to consolidate your out-of-control credit card debt?*" I cringed on the spot for that couple.

Regardless of the type of business you are in, people value their privacy, perhaps now more than ever. They want to be able to feel emotionally secure when they share what they want and why.

In many professions, they may be sharing their fears, uncertainties, and doubts. No one wants to do that in a place that offers little to no privacy. The open architecture of many sales organizations and stores does give some pause and makes people feel concerned that those in the next booth over can hear them.

The same is true of meeting in a public place. Think from their perspective: Would you like others to hear your private concerns?

To this same end, be mindful of your conference room and how it is designed. Does it afford privacy?

Yes, you might close the door, but if you have a glass wall that faces out into the hallway and clients are seated facing that glass wall, all those passing by in the hall can see them.

Once when I was in New Jersey at an office, a woman abruptly stood up in a glass conference room and said, "*This setting is unacceptable. My neighbors can see me in here if they walk by and they will know I have a lot of money.*"

To avoid this happening to you, have the clients face into the room so they are not easily seen or distracted.

Remember it isn't what you think that matters. What matters is what you can do to make them emotionally secure.

Finally, call the spaces where you meet people conference rooms, not meeting rooms. Conference rooms suggest that we are conferring and having a conversation. Or you may wish to do as Carson Wealth in Omaha does. They take it a step further and call their conference spaces "conversation rooms." Delightful positioning and imaging!

TACTIC 35: PROACTIVELY PROVIDE CLIENTS WITH AN EMERGENCY CONTACT NUMBER

Many large companies have customer service lines that people can call after normal business hours. Online, there are real time AI and chat systems in place for clients when they want to reach out. And, of course, during business hours they can call directly to a place of business and reach someone.

However, life doesn't run on a schedule. That is why many of the trade service companies have 24/7/365 emergency hotline numbers, a mainstay of their business.

If your plumbing springs a leak, you can call. If your heating or A/C goes out, you can call. Even if you need your doctor in an emergency, you can usually call their office and get connected to their paging service.

So, what happens to your clients in an emergency or an unexpected situation, such as a major storm? Can they reach you or a member of your team, or do they need to wait for your office hours to reach you?

You can really build emotional connection and currency when you offer your clients a defined way of contacting you in an emergency or unexpected situation.

Proactively give them your cell phone number as "*their emergency hotline number.*" If you just say, "here is my cell number," we have found in our client advocacy assessment work that they will still be reluctant to call, as they don't want to "bother you." However, interestingly, if you position your cell as their emergency hotline number, they will save it and use it if there is an emergency. Positioning matters!

Also, if you have several people in your organization who could take the client call, do what the trades do. They get a dedicated phone number, such as the type that Google and others offer, and publish it as their emergency hotline number. They then forward those calls to the "on call" technician for that day and/or time. You can and should do the same. Give your emergency hotline number to your clients proactively. It builds significant emotional security while demonstrating that you really are there for them.

TACTIC 36: IF YOU MAKE A MISTAKE, APOLOGIZE

People in general are very forgiving. They know that none of us is perfect. They realize mistakes happen, and as long as the same mistake does not keep happening to them, they appreciate a true apology. When you apologize sincerely, they will most likely accept it and then want to move one. However, some people have a hard time apologizing for anything. Narcissism kicks in and their apology isn't an apology at all. We all have experienced this. It usually begins with "I am sorry *if…*" which is not an apology. It is an expression that really says, "I doubt I did anything wrong."

A sincere apology requires taking responsibility. "I apologize *for…*" will win people over and help all move forward in the relationship.

And in case you are wondering, saying *"my bad"* is not a real apology; it is simply the same as *"oh, sorry if I…"*

TACTIC 37: FOCUS ON SHOWING THEM HOW INSTEAD OF WHAT

Most love the technology we have available to serve and illustrate things for clients. Regardless of what type of business you have, many clients can log in online and check the status of almost anything you are doing for them. They can process all or nearly all paperwork from their location and not have to come into your office for routine things. However, not all clients are technology savvy.

Yes, they can be told what to do to access and use the technology, but some need more hands-on support. They need step-by-step guidance on *how* to do it.

I have heard many stories of some clients who don't know how to log in or who refuse to use electronic signature because they don't know what it is or how it works.

Don't just tell clients to register for your online portal. Take the time to walk them through it step by step in person or through screen sharing so they are comfortable navigating the site. When a client can't use the technology you provide, it creates emotional stress and discouragement. Don't let that happen—ever.

TACTIC 38: PROACTIVELY LET THEM KNOW WHO TO CALL

No matter what industry you are in, clients need direction on who to call for what.

I suggest you create a "Who to Contact" document that details who to call for what. "Need a balance? Call …" "Need a transfer? Call…" "Need advice? Call…" "Need an appointment? Call…" "Need a showing? Call…" "Need a plumber? Call…" and so on.

This document should have headshots of your team members, along with their phone and email information. This increases responsiveness, improves efficiency, reduces client anxiety, and makes it easy for clients to do business with you. Give this document to them the first time they meet with you to demonstrate that you are organized, efficient, caring, and thoughtful. This approach removes their concerns upfront and helps them feel emotionally engaged and connected with you.

TACTIC 39: HAVE AN AGENDA FOR MAJOR MEETINGS AND CONVERSATIONS

People like to know what is going to be covered at a high level when they confer with you. This helps them organize their thoughts and prepare anything they need to bring with them. An agenda also enables the discussion to run smoothly and ensure that nothing important is overlooked or forgotten. Unless the meeting or visit is informal, I suggest you send the agenda to the client or prospective client in advance via email.

This tells them subliminally that you are thinking of them and care that the time spent is beneficial for them. The first item on any agenda, as I will detail in a subsequent tip, should be *What are three things you are interested in discussing or exploring when we are together?*

I suggested to a financial advisor that he include this as the first item on the agenda for an upcoming first consultation with a prospective client. The client sent back a six-page email detailing the things he wanted to discuss. That completely changed the direction of that discussion, and the advisor was able to engage with this individual as a major client.

TACTIC 40: BE REALISTIC IN YOUR RESPONSIVENESS

In today's competitive market, response time is an important key to client advocacy and clients' sense of being cared for. They expect that you will respond to their inquiries quickly and efficiently.

Unfortunately, in the sales and service process it is easy to unrealistically promise more than you or your firm can deliver. It is better to say, *"I will be sure you have this within twenty-four hours and notify you when it is done"* than to say, *"We will get this out today"* and then not follow through. That broken promise will upset and frustrate clients.

To prevent this from happening, provide clients with an honest assessment of what they can expect and when. If you promise something and delay delivery more than once, people will get frustrated and feel taken for granted. Emotional security erodes when promised time frames are missed.

TACTIC 41: BE DEFINITIVE—IT BUILDS THEIR CONFIDENCE

As I have illustrated several times, words matter. In conversation with a client, when you are answering a question, making a recommendation, or giving directions, be definitive. It is reasonable to say that when you seem unsure, they will be too. So, avoid noncommittal words. It is better to say "Let me get back to you when I can give you a definite answer" than to be noncommittal, which erodes both their emotional and economic sense of security.

Avoid	Use
I think	I know
I might	I will
I probably	I definitely
I guess	I am sure
I am not sure	I don't know

CHAPTER 4

HOW TO MAKE CLIENTS AND PROSPECTS FEEL SECURE ECONOMICALLY

Critical to providing economic security is demonstrating thoughtfulness, empathy, and patience when you engage in discovery.

One of the things that destroys a client or prospective client's desire to embrace a solution and their sense that you will treat them right is if you are perceived as "pushy." Being pushy means that you are all about your product or service and not focusing on or listening to them.

How you react during early discovery can be another turnoff. If you prejudge them as buyers, they will feel as though you don't believe they have accomplished enough financially to afford (i.e., qualify) to own the product or service they seek.

To combat these negative responses and ensure that they don't occur, be measured in your approach.

Instead of jumping right into discovery, think first about their frame of mind. As mentioned in a previous chapter, people, even existing clients, can and often do have fear, uncertainty, or doubt about what to do or if they should even spend or invest the money.

Consequently, people first want to feel and sense your thoughtfulness, your interest in and empathy for their situation. When they feel this, they are far more inclined to tell you what they want to do, listen to you, and do business with you. Emotionally they will have a powerful sense that doing business with you is the right economic decision for them.

To achieve this, you want to discover what it is that brought them to you today and what outcome they desire to have.

Brandon Carson, Walmart's VP of Learning and Leadership, posted a great story about this on LinkedIn. He was at Apple creating sales training during Steve Job's tenure and a bit post-Steve creating sales training. He says they didn't have an explicit "sales model" for the iPhone or iPad like most companies. As he stated, "We believed in telling the story of how our products were designed for what the customer values the most, then showed them how easy it was to do it with an Apple product."

His illustration of how they did this is spot on:

> *If someone said, "I want to send and receive photos of my grandchildren," we would then show them how iPad would enable them to DO that. And we would let them do it.*

He further stated:

> *Apple taught me that selling technology is never about product features and specifications. It's always about what the person wants to do. The technology is just the means to the end…and the end is always something to do with people. It's a simple process of ensuring that you always place the focus on the customer and what they value the most.*

Another great example of understanding first what people want and what brought them to you is that of two financial advisors who met a wealthy couple in their hotel suite. To their credit, they engaged both the husband

and wife in an empathetic and thoughtful way. They began by asking the couple what they wanted to discuss.

The wife spoke first about what was important to her. For a solid half hour, she shared her real concerns on how to pass their estate to their many grandchildren. When she was done, she stopped and said, *"Thank you for taking the time to hear me out and for taking such good notes."* She then turned to her husband and said, *"Honey, I think these gentlemen really can help us."* And in the end, they did bring them on as high-net-worth clients.

Both stories illustrate that to demonstrate value and provide economic security to your clients, you need to understand their perspective. They want to feel confident that you want to know what is important to them and specifically what they want to solve, enjoy, or experience through you and your offerings.

Simply put, people want to feel confident that you are there for them and not just for yourself. To demonstrate that, consistently use these tactics to assure them that they are in the right place with the right professional and company.

TACTIC 42: START EVERY MEETING OFF ON THEIR FOOTING, NOT YOURS

Regardless of whether you are providing professional services or a product like home alarm systems or a new car, start every discussion with a client or prospective client with *"What are three things you are interested in discussing or exploring today?"*

This simple opening question reassures them that you are not all about you but, rather, that you care about them and what they wish to accomplish.

Yes, you may have things you need to cover with an existing client in a meeting; however, a great deal of business is lost because clients (and prospective clients) do not have the opportunity to get their questions answered.

I was on an elevator recently when a couple got on, and before the door was even closed, she turned to him and said, *"Why didn't you tell him we wanted to refinance the house?"* His response was, *"They were very busy, and he said he had a lot to cover with us, so I never had a chance."* She said, *"That's it—we need to find another lender, as it is clear these people don't have time for us."*

Candidly, it does not matter if you ever get through your agenda, but you had better be sure they get through theirs!

TACTIC 43: UNCOVER DEEP-SEATED WORRIES AND SOLUTION WILLINGNESS

People have a natural tendency to be guarded about the things that concern them the most. They can also be guarded about their willingness to find solutions lest they seem too eager and get your most convenient solution instead of the best one.

To demonstrate that you are there for *them*, and to give them the confidence to be transparent, use emotionally engaging Trilogy Questions™ instead of simple tactical and binary ones.

Here are a few Trilogy Questions that are thoughtful, emotionally engaging, and that will uncover deep concerns and willingness to solve.

They will also help you understand the client's perspective and how they think before making any recommendations.

To uncover and engage their passions:

1. *If there were three things you could spend time doing now or in the future, what would they be?*

2. *What three things do you want to do with your money to leave a legacy or make a difference?*

To seek and find areas of concern:

1. *What are the three issues that are on your mind regarding this purchase/decision/issue?*

2. *If there were three outcomes you would hope to achieve by working together, what would they be?* (**Note:** Use outcomes, rather than things, in this question to determine what result they value.)

To determine willingness to solve:

1. *What are three things you would like to do now to ensure you can buy the home of your dreams?* (This probes their priorities.)

2. *What are three things that we haven't discussed yet?*

Our experience as coaches and consultants is that most of the time when using Trilogy Questions, the third thing that a client wants to discuss is the most critical and the one that *must* be resolved.

Use one, or no more than two, Trilogy Questions in any discussion to be seen as a caring solver!

TACTIC 44: DON'T JUMP—BE SLOW TO RESPOND

When Lexus first came to the USA, they taught their sales teams to probe empathetically, and it gave them a strong foothold in the marketplace that remains today. As soon as a customer walked into a showroom, the first question typically was *"Why do you want to buy a Lexus?"* followed by the empathetic *"Who do you want to buy it for?"*

Why is this demonstration of thoughtfulness and empathy important?

As a sales and service professional, you often know the solution before the client has even fully revealed the issue they want to solve. Consequently, the tendency is to jump on the first thing they want to discuss instead of waiting for a full reveal from the client.

Don't jump—just listen, hold your comments, and then probe their answers further and more deeply. Demonstrate empathy for them, and you will achieve fuller and deeper discovery with phrases and questions such as:

> *Tell me more about that…*
> *How do you feel about that?*
> *How has that affected things?*
> *Why do you feel that way?*
> *What impact does/will that have on…*

Once you have this additional clarity, repeat what they say they want and say something like, *"So, if I understand you correctly, you want to make sure Lucy has enough money to be cared for and not be a burden to your other two children, correct?"*

Remember Steven Covey's second habit: Begin with the end in mind. If you can agree with what the client wants to achieve, it is easier to focus on the strategies to reach the goal. Simply put, when you find out what they really want and why, you both win.

TACTIC 45: BE SURE TO EXPLAIN WHAT THEY WILL ACCOMPLISH

In my last book, *The Power of Why: Breaking Out in a Competitive Marketplace* (available on Amazon in several languages), I wrote extensively on how to communicate your value from the buyer/client point of view. It is essential that you slow down and speak in plain language about how your recommendations will solve their issue.

The fact remains that far too many clients leave because they don't understand the value of your expertise, your product, your services, or your recommendations.

Just because you know the value of you and your work, it doesn't mean they do unless you make it crystal clear.

Tell them about your recommendation, your product, or your service, and then tell them, *"and what this means for you is…"* so they will understand how it applies to their situation. By communicating from their perspective, you reinforce in their mind that you are there for them and not for yourself, and you give them a true sense of economic as well as emotional security.

TACTIC 46: AVOID TALKING DOWN TO THEM

No matter how much emotional currency you have with a client, it will be worthless if they feel like you are demeaning or disrespecting them by talking down to them.

Unfortunately, this happens far too often in all types of conversations—not just in sales or service conversations but even with friends and family whenever we are attempting to tell a story, describe something, or explain something. The worst part is that most of us don't realize we are doing it because of a lack of awareness of the words we use.

Asking someone after you describe or explain, *"Does that make sense?"* or *"Are you with me?"* can be perceived as saying "are you smart enough to keep up?" *Ouch!*

It is far better to own the responsibility of making it clear by asking *"Did I explain that clearly?"*

Another unconscious put-down I hear often is the preface, *"I know this is complicated and hard to understand..."* Ouch again!

If it is complicated, it is your job as a professional to break it down and make it uncomplicated.

Also don't ask *"Do you have any questions?"* The way to solicit their input in a gracious, relational way is instead to ask them, *"What questions do you have so far?"*

TACTIC 47: ANY COMMUNICATION THAT TELLS THEM THEY ARE WRONG WILL NOT BE RECEIVED

One of our financial services clients recorded and sent us an initial meeting he had with a prospect to see where he could improve. His initial rapport building, although not very personalized, did break the ice and engage the prospect. To his credit, he uncovered some important topics of concern to the prospect.

But then the advisor said, "*Well, let me tell you what your problem is and what you and **the advisor you are working with** are doing wrong,*" then delivered a litany about "*not having the right plan, too many of the wrong investments, and no real knowledge of market opportunities.*"

At the end of this speech by the advisor, the prospect said in an adamant tone, "*This meeting is over. I thought you were here to solve my problems, but instead all you want to do is point out what I am doing wrong and blame me and my current advisor for them.*"

So, what can you learn from this?

1. First and foremost, always attack the problem, not the person.

2. Position yourself as a problem solver, not a fault finder.

3. Be keenly aware that what you say matters most to the person who hears it.

Here is how to implement these three key learnings:

> *Okay, it is clear we have several issues we can work on together to solve. You have a plan now that needs some review and revamping. You have some investments that need to be looked at given the current market conditions and the direction you want your financial future to take. What else is important to you besides these issues?*

This approach raises issues as a list to be further assessed and then solved.

Be mindful that any communication that tells people they are wrong will not be received! So, be a solver and not the judge and jury.

TACTIC 48: THE PHRASE THAT DESTROYS ECONOMIC AND EMOTIONAL SECURITY AND TRUST

If there is one phrase that always erodes confidence, it is: *"Let me be honest with you."* We all have heard it, we may even have used it, and we all know that it doesn't mean we haven't been honest. Yes, knowing that you have been honest all along may be your excuse for using it, but how would the client know that?

Anything that erodes or destroys a client's perception that you are not being fully transparent erodes trust and their sense of emotional and economic security. Instead of *"Let me be honest with you"* when they have a question or concern, say, *"Here is how this works."*

TACTIC 49: AVOID "WITH ALL DUE RESPECT"

While clients will sometimes disagree with you, avoid using the passive aggressive approach of saying, *"Okay, I understand what you're saying but with all due respect, I…"* Not only do those words create defensiveness in those who hear them, but also, and worse, what the listener really hears is, *"I actually don't respect what you are saying."*

Instead, be gracious and say something like *"While I see your point, I don't agree with you, and here is why."* You must be willing to explain your view without degrading or diminishing theirs. If you don't, you will damage their relationship with you and erode their emotional and economic security. This will likely cause them to ponder your comment and ask themselves *am I in the right place with the right professional?*

TACTIC 50: IF ONLY YOU HAD A BRAIN, THIS WOULD BE THE PERFECT SOLUTION

I recently received an email from a commercial real estate broker lamenting how he had lost a great prospective client. He had worked hard to get this individual interested in purchasing a rental property in Buffalo, NY. After several discussions, the buyer said it was not the right time. Six months later he reengaged with the broker about another property. The broker said, *"I was moving him along in the process and then I happened to mention the first property I showed him six months before. I told him he should have bought it as it was a deal and a 'no brainer.'"*

The buyer immediately said, *"Really, it was a no brainer? I don't do business with people who are so arrogant that they think I am stupid."*

Well, there you go—let's be judgmental and then use slang that runs the prospect into the ground! *Not* such a lovely experience.

TACTIC 51: REASSURE THEM AND DON'T PRESUME ANYTHING

Clients are always the best source of more business. Unfortunately, many clients don't realize the scope and breadth of what you can do for them. Few actually know all the services and solutions you offer.

This is evidenced by the sad stories we all have heard about a client who bought somewhere else and said, *"Oh, I didn't know you sold that too."*

Regardless of your type of business, you build economic security, as well as emotional security, with people by informing them that you are a resource for all their needs within your area of expertise.

Take time to articulate examples to clients and prospective clients of what you have done for others so they can see you are truly a resource for them as well.

When they see you as a true resource, they will demonstrate that by calling you first when they have a question or desire in your area of expertise. This beats them calling your competitor.

This also works in reverse. Position your client as a resource for another client. If you have a client who is a commercial real estate broker who could be helpful to a client with a manufacturing facility who needs to expand, put them together. They will undoubtedly share with others how thoughtful you are and how much you helped them.

TACTIC 52: ALWAYS REFERENCE NEXT STEPS

No matter how well you articulate and explain the value you deliver, people need help moving forward.

People want to know the next steps to take to do business with you. Why?

You can't ride a bike, drive a car, run a mile, lose a pound, or get engaged to marry until you take a step. People seek and appreciate "next steps" so they understand what is expected of them and what they can expect from you. They want to see the path forward that you are providing.

An excellent way to state this is to say, *"Here are the next steps we are going to take on your behalf..."*

That phrase has proven to demonstrate thoughtfulness, empathy, kindness, and caring to clients and prospective clients. They are thrilled that finally someone is doing something on their behalf to help them get what they want and desire.

This phrase is often mentioned when people describe or mention to you why working with you is such an elevated experience. *"You are always doing things on our behalf."*

No amount of marketing can beat that advocacy on *your* behalf.

This same reference to next steps works for online inquiries as well. Simply state, *"Please feel welcome to contact us for more information on the steps needed to [install, see, find, have, etc.]."*

TACTIC 53: NEAR THE END OF THE MEETING, TREAT IT LIKE THE BEGINNING

When the meeting or conversation is winding down and all agenda items have been covered, clients still may have something to discuss that is not on the agenda. We have found that asking *"Is there anything else?"* typically does not uncover "other" issues. Why? It is the wrong question because people often think that you are asking about what was on the agenda. They have nothing else to ask about that.

However, they may have another important topic that needs to be discussed. Ask them: *"What other topics or issues are on your mind to discuss today, if any?"* You will often discover other very real and important items they never mentioned.

TACTIC 54: ALWAYS CLOSE EVERY CONVERSATION, REGARDLESS OF BREVITY, BY REINFORCING THAT YOU CARE

Years ago, when I was in the Rolls-Royce business, I discovered quite by accident a way to tell my clients or prospective clients "you matter." At the very end of a telephone conversation or meeting, I said, *"What else can I do for you today?"* Often, there was nothing else that they needed or wanted, but they nearly always said, *"I appreciate that, thank you!"* That simple question not only demonstrates that you care but also says "I value you, you have my undivided attention, and I am not too busy for you"—a priceless image to plant in their mind.

TACTIC 55: STOP "FOLLOWING UP"

For prospective clients or clients who have not yet decided to move forward, a common approach is to call them or email them and say, *"I am following up to see what decision you have made."*

Please *stop*.

"Following up" is a meaningless phrase and suggests there is no more you can add to help them in their decision process. Besides, if they had already made a decision, it is very likely they would have called you!

So, when you call or email them, instead of "following up," use this approach:

> *I am calling/writing to discuss some additional steps I have identified that we can take together to [get that dream home you want, get your financial life in balance, increase your protection, set up a college fund, afford that remodel, etc.].*

The more specific you are about naming how you can help them accomplish what they seek, the deeper will be their desire to take the next step. When you tell them you have identified additional steps, you are reinforcing your value and your ability to help them. This speaks loudly to them that you are thinking about them, care about them, and want to help them achieve what they want. It gives them both the emotional and economic security they seek.

TACTIC 56: WHAT TO DO WHEN THEY SAY NO INSTEAD OF YES!

You have done a great job uncovering the needs and wants of a prospective client. You have communicated your value from their perspective. You have answered every question. You have been very clear about what you can and will do on their behalf.

Yet some still say no.

There can be many reasons for clients to say no, from *"I am not ready to do all this"* to *"I don't think we really have enough to do this right now"* to *"this just isn't a good time."*

In cases like this, it is important to realize that instead of writing them off, you should cultivate them. Timing is everything.

To cultivate them:

1. Treat them like people who have already bought. If they are a prospective client, enroll them in your database and keep them informed on their topics of interest.

2. As soon as they say no, send them a handwritten thank-you note for saying no. Not an email, but a handwritten note which makes a powerful and memorable impact. The note should say something like this:

   Hi first name(s),

   I am disappointed we are unable to work together now to help you build a plan for the retirement you rightly deserve. However, I look forward to working with you in the future.

   Always feel welcome to call.
   Warmest regards,

The words matter in this note. Don't write *I am sorry*; rather, be *disappointed*. Don't write *I hope*; rather, *I look forward*. Don't write *feel free*; rather, *feel welcome*.

What this says to the prospective client is that, although your solution was not feasible at this time, you are still here for them. You can also use this approach with clients who are reluctant to move forward on something they need or want.

When I had the idea to begin sending thank-you notes for saying no, I was surprised at the immediate results that followed. It is simply amazing how readily many prospective clients feel comfortable reengaging. Some reengage immediately, some might in six months or even a year, and some never will. But by sending a thoughtful note to thank them for saying no, combined with treating them like the valuable people they are, you will be richly rewarded.

CHAPTER 5

HOW TO KNOW YOUR CLIENTS AND PROSPECTS BETTER AND BUILD A ROCK-SOLID RELATIONSHIP

Relationships are the bedrock of a sustainable business. Strong, nurtured relationships create advocacy, generate referrals, drive revenue, build positive name recognition, and foster a deep sense of emotional engagement and connection with clients. In the absence of a rock-solid relationship, clients may be satisfied but they are too often willing to look for and turn to another professional or company.

People today want to work with an individual who is focused on them and wants to know and understand them as a person and as part of a family.

People are tired of being treated like a number, and, as I mentioned in a previous chapter, they don't want to be seen as an account. With the advent of social media, many feel the loss of a real relational connection to other people.

Contrary to some opinions in the marketplace, social media platforms can be useful in building relationships with clients and prospects *if* the focus is on them as people, as I have addressed previously.

The bedrock of successful relationships is formed by knowledge, empathy, thoughtfulness, caring, and kindness. Knowing who your clients and prospects are, their point of view, what they enjoy, and what they desire is fundamental to the development of a rock-solid relationship that will withstand the stressful waves of the marketplace and of life.

These tactics will help you know them better, and, as a result, they will realize that you truly are there for them and you will gain their respect and advocacy.

A word of caution: Avoid the common belief that people will not share things about themselves with you. This is simply not true.

Brad Davis, CEO of DataLucent, provides real insight confirming that people will share things about themselves. "*A customer's willingness to share deep information about themselves is fundamentally about their level of affinity with a brand.*"

Milton Pedraza, CEO of the Luxury Institute, states: "*First-party customer data access is the lifeblood of all mass, premium or luxury brands. It defines the customer relationship, perhaps more than transactions or recommendations.*"

When you approach relationship building with the mindset of caring, empathy, thoughtfulness, and kindness, people *will* share their lives with you. All you must do is *ask.*

TACTIC 57: TREAT YOUR CRM AS A CXM (CLIENT EXPERIENCE MANAGER)

Data points are most often viewed as transactional, but capturing the right data makes them experiential. By focusing on people as individuals and not just as a transaction or as an account, you will uncover ways to consistently elevate their experience with you.

Unfortunately, the gap in understanding that professionals have about what their clients enjoy, have done, will do, and are doing is massive. Evaluate yourself by thinking of your top five clients and answering the following questions:

- *What are their recreational interests?*
- *Where did they and where do their children go to school?*
- *How are they involved in the community?*
- *Did they serve in the military?*

How about your next five clients?

People love to talk about their interests and their involvement when someone takes the time to ask them. Unfortunately, many clients are lost because of the lack of knowledge about them, which in their minds translates to the belief that you aren't interested.

Case in point: During the pandemic, a wealthy couple were invited to a virtual bourbon tasting by their longtime financial advisor.

They graciously declined and told the advisor that they do not drink for religious reasons. Fast forward to the first summer of in-person events. They received an invitation from their advisor for a wine tasting to be followed by a market briefing. Once again, they declined and asked not to be invited to these types of events. Fast forward to the holiday season, and the branch sends them an invite for cocktails to meet the senior leadership of the firm.

They did not decline this invitation. They moved to another firm within a week. When I spoke to the advisor about how this happened and how to prevent this in the future, he said, *"Well, we put it in their account notes and just missed it."*

In today's technological environment, preferences need to be in your system as their own search field, not in your notes. After all, who searches notes for preferences?

The way forward is to treat your Customer Relationship Manager (CRM) as a Client Experience Manager (CXM). Set up fields on beverages clients (and prospects) prefer, events they enjoy, recreational interests, charitable interests, educational interests, and a field to codify what they say they *do not like.*

Without this knowledge, you miss opportunities to relate, and you run the risk of offending. Capturing relational data in today's technological world is and should be a constant focus of your ongoing interactions.

People love to feel significant, and that happens when you take the time to know them better. As detailed in the next tactic, the more you know, the stronger and more meaningful the relationship will be.

TACTIC 58: ONBOARDING—KNOW THEIR WHAT AND THEIR WHERE

One of the great and often missed opportunities to develop new client relationships is during the *onboarding process*, or, as I suggest you call it from now on, the *welcoming process*. This renaming will help you to stay focused on gracious, thoughtful, empathetic steps and engagement.

Many important decisions and assessments are made when welcoming a new client. When you welcome a new client, regardless of what product or services you sell, it is an ideal time to gather insight that will help you build a relationship.

However, this opportunity to strengthen relationships (and marketing opportunities) can easily be lost during this initial engagement unless you detail it in the welcoming process.

Every client is proud of, involved in, or interested in certain things. We all have heard that knowledge is power. To amplify that statement, the more you know, the greater the power.

Several years ago, I was at Bergdorf Goodman in NYC. My wife was purchasing a bathrobe for a six-year-old grandson. The sales assistant was very gracious and engaged. She asked who the robe was for. What was his name? When was his birthday? What was his favorite type of toy and sport? The conversation flowed in a smooth and relaxed way as the purchase was completed. A week later, my wife received a thank-you note from the sales assistant at Bergdorf Goodman. Better still, each year for several years as the boy's birthday approached, my wife received an email with suggestions for birthday gifts based on his love of trains and baseball. Needless to say, they got a lot more of our business.

So, how about you? When you welcome people into your business, do you have a relational checklist that prompts you to ask and capture key information? Here are just a few of the items that need to be on that checklist, and please note that these questions should be presented in a conversational manner with care given to gauge the client's comfort level and ensure that they do not feel pressured to answer.

What organizations do you belong to that support what you do for a living?

What recreational clubs do you belong to, or what recreational things do you enjoy doing?

What are your cultural, charitable, ethnic, and religious affiliations or interests?

What are your favorite social activities?

Did you serve in the military?

When is your wedding anniversary?

What is your favorite adult beverage?

What are your favorite sports to watch and which teams?

What is your favorite snack food?

What type of car do you drive?

What are your pets' names?

What are your children's/grandchildren's names?

What is your preferred method of contact?

What is generally the best time to call you?

What prompted you to leave your other provider?

Why did you select us/me as your new provider?

Make no mistake, people love to talk about their family, interests, and involvements and will be thrilled that you are interested.

A financial advisor with nearly thirty years in the business heard me speak about this tactic and took it to heart. He realized he had a large knowledge gap regarding his clients. Though reluctant, he finally called his top five and inquired about their interests and involvements. He said, *"These were the best calls I have EVER made."*

Capturing these key data points as you welcome them, and continue to capture them over time, strengthens your knowledge of and relationship with them. It provides you with nearly unlimited ways to elevate their experience, create emotional engagement and personalize and humanize their touch points with you.

TACTIC 59: CONTINUE TO BE CURIOUS ABOUT THEIR CURRENT INTERESTS AND ACTIVITIES

Things change. Activities and interests change. To help you keep your CXM data up to date and your relationship on track, be curious and listen for opportunities to know more. As an example, when you meet a client or prospect, after you greet them with *"nice to see you"* and they greet you as well, ask them *"What are you (and the family) most excited about this [year, spring, holiday, etc.]?"*

Wow—what an experiential data-gathering opportunity that will be! It will be great to capture in your CXM so that you can inquire about their new activities later.

TACTIC 60: DEMONSTRATE YOUR INTEREST IN WHAT THEY SEE OR HAVE SEEN

People have many things that they want to accomplish or feel proud about completing.

In a casual, conversational way over time, ask your clients and prospects one of the following, using the preface *"I admire you"* or *"I am curious…"*

- *What are you most proud of in your life?*
- *What is your greatest accomplishment so far?*
- *What are some other things you still want to do in your life?*

Capture their answers in your CXM so you can refer back to what they are most proud of, their greatest accomplishment, and/or what they still want to do. I have received many emails from professionals saying that this simple relational tactic not only further solidified their client relationships but also resulted in a much stronger emotional bond with clients.

TACTIC 61: CONNECT WITH YOUR CLIENTS AND PROSPECTS ON THEIR SOCIAL MEDIA PLATFORMS

The usual mindset regarding the use of social media is that it should be used to promote yourself and your business. This is fine, of course. Done right, it drives inquiries and revenue.

However, the most overlooked use of social media is to help your clients and prospects know that you are following and supporting them. Connect with all your best clients and target prospects on any social media platform they use that you have access to. By connecting, you will be able to see their postings and stay relevant to their situation.

Be sure to comment on their posts, as people often post for visibility and recognition. However, avoid non-relational autoreplies such as "Congrats!" Instead, spell it out with their name: "Congratulations, Ellen!" This way, the recipient will know you are sincere and not just going through the motions.

In addition, reshare your best clients' and prospects' posts, and tag them when you do. This tells them instantly that you are there for them! We have done this for years, and the results are gratifying. Clients appreciate the support and see you as a friend of their family and their network. Powerful imaging!

TACTIC 62: USE YOUR SOCIAL MEDIA AS A RELATIONSHIP TOOL, NOT JUST A LEAD SOURCE

I have asked many people, *"What is the real reason to be on social media for business?"* The answers I hear most often, in hierarchal order, are:

1. *To get appointments.*

2. *To find and sell more prospects.*

3. *To create connections.*

While these reasons may seem valid at some level, I kindly suggest these three reasons to be on social media for business:

1. To create and enhance relationships.

2. To become recognized as a knowledgeable resource for your connections/followers.

3. To create interest and curiosity about how you help people solve their issues.

Consider Alan Cohen's famous message: *"Success in business depends more on relationships than spreadsheets."*

With that in mind, here are a few simple yet powerful tips to maximize your social media image:

1. Avoid "Connect and Pitch"!

2. Thank them for connecting. Tell them you look forward to viewing their content.

3. Start liking and engaging their content. It's a slower process, but far more effective and relational than baiting and switching with sales pitches.

4. Follow the organizations your prospects and clients are in so you can be informed and relationally proactive.

TACTIC 63: USE GOOGLE TO STAY RELEVANT AND INFORMED

For your best clients (and prospects), set up a Google Alert on them, their industry, their company, their profession, their networks, and their interests. To set up an alert, simply navigate to google.com/alerts in your web browser, type in the name or phrase you want Google to search for and click "Create Alert." To customize the search, click "Show options." From there, you can select the frequency and sources for the search, where to send the results, and more. Then, magically, if that person or phrase appears anywhere online, you will get a notification in your inbox. *Wow!* And it costs exactly nothing, which is another *wow*.

This information will keep you in the loop on the market and the people you are doing business with and will strengthen your relationship with them.

TACTIC 64: FORWARD APPROPRIATE GOOGLE ALERTS TO YOUR BEST CLIENTS AND PROSPECTS

After you set up your Google Alerts per the previous tactic and are keeping yourself in the loop on your clients and markets, be sure to also use the alerts as a relationship-building tool.

Send appropriate alerts via email to your clients (and prospective clients) and tell them *"I thought you would enjoy seeing this."* You will be amazed at how many times a client or even a prospective client will reply graciously to something you send and with genuine appreciation that you sent it.

Don't let negative thinking get in the way here by thinking that they may have already seen what you send. What matters is that you thought of them when you saw it and cared enough to send it!

When you send items of interest proactively to them, it creates awareness that you're thinking of them, and this positions you as a resource in touch with the things they care about. Most importantly, it elevates their experience and strengthens your relationship with them and theirs with you.

TACTIC 65: LEARN MORE BY WALKING THEM ALL THE WAY OUT

When a meeting is over, the common practice is to walk a client to the office lobby or to the elevator. Some even have a staff person walk people to the elevator or the lobby as they perceive themselves to be "too busy."

What I have learned is that when *you* take the few extra steps to walk out with them, the relational dynamics change instantly. Clients are more relaxed when they are out of your office or conference space. Ride the elevator down with them to the main floor.

They will tell you things in the elevator that they would likely never mention in your office. If you're on the ground floor, walk them through the lobby to the building entrance and say goodbye to them.

The extra steps you take demonstrate that they are important to you and that you have time to invest in them and the relationship. I recently heard from a young man who walked his clients all the way to their car in the garage. They not only told him what they were doing for the weekend but said they had forgotten to tell him their son was thinking of buying a beach house and wondered if he could help with the financing.

TACTIC 66: AVOID MAKING DONATIONS ON YOUR CLIENT'S BEHALF

In our busy, fast-paced environment, sometimes when a holiday arises or a client is celebrating something, you might think *"I need to do something, but I just don't have time."*

Consequently, you might make a donation on the client's behalf to your favorite charity or one that you feel is innocuous enough to not be an issue. Contrary to what you may think, however, you should never, ever donate on your client's behalf unless they ask you to do so.

I have heard many horror stories from people who were offended that a gift was made on their behalf to an organization or cause that they did not and would not support. Doing nothing is better than assuming that unsolicited donations will be appreciated.

TACTIC 67: DEMONSTRATE YOUR VALUES IN YOUR WORDS AND ACTIONS

To build long-lasting relationships with clients, remember that they want to know *you*, not just what you do for them. Clients are keenly interested in your values, your interests, and what you are passionate about.

They are tired of people who they believe are just going through the motions and are not really caring, kind, thoughtful, and empathetic people doing the best that is possible for them.

When you demonstrate your values in your words and actions, people will find that they can relate to you. To this point, I was asked at a meeting in London, *"What is the most important thing needed for people to determine if they could have a relationship with you?"*

My answer was *"Be genuine,"* and then I defined genuine straight out of my Oxford dictionary written in the early 1800s: *Not counterfeit.*

To win more business and create sustainable relationships in this hyper-competitive environment, demonstrate your authenticity and values over sales talk and persona.

TACTIC 68: PAY ATTENTION AND AVOID UPSTAGING THEM

Once a client knows you and is comfortable, they often will tell you stories that will help you know them better. Having them share their stories and experiences with you is one of the great joys of relationship building and emotional bonding.

When they are telling their stories, be sure to do these two things:

1. Listen and give them your undivided attention. What they tell you is important to them, and you want to demonstrate that it is important to you as well. When you demonstrate curiosity about what they are sharing, they will feel more confident that they can tell you anything, and from my experience, they will. As they share, ask for more of their story: "*Who were you with?*" "*What did you think?*" "*How did you feel?*" "*Where was this?*" These simple yet thoughtful phrases demonstrate that you are listening and show relational curiosity.

2. Avoid upstaging their story with one of your own on the same or a similar topic. Remember that the goal is to make them feel comfortable to share their stories with you so you can know them better. So, avoid upstaging them. Upstaging can shift clients to the mindset that you aren't really interested in their stories *or* in them.

TACTIC 69: ANNUALLY CAPTURE ADDITIONAL WAYS TO ELEVATE THEIR RELATIONSHIP WITH YOU

Given that client satisfaction surveys only look backward, they give no real tactical input on where or how you can proactively improve. So, instead of satisfaction surveys, ask your clients at least once a year: *"What else can I/we do to elevate your experience with me/us?"* By asking this question in a positive and expectant tone of voice, you will get good insight. Most importantly, be mindful of these three things.

1. Whatever they share, capture it, and thank them for it.

2. Think creatively about how you can implement their suggestion.

    Example: A good friend asked his widowed client, *"What else can we do to elevate your experience with us?"* She replied, *"I hate driving here in all the traffic, and I am sick of virtual meetings. It just isn't very fulfilling, as I don't get to see the rest of your lovely staff."* That got him thinking—how many others felt that way about the traffic and virtual meetings? To address the issue, he partnered with one of his clients that owns a local car service. He now offers all his widowed clients as well as several of his executives' complimentary car service to and from meetings.

    Sure, they could use Uber or Lyft, but by proactively offering the service he wins their admiration, elevates their experience, and creates delighted advocates.

3. If for some reason it is not possible to act on their suggestion, only tell them that after you thoroughly research how you could possibly implement it. This shows that you have sincerely considered their suggestion and would have acted on it if it had been possible. This is far better than immediately judging their comments or suggestions with *"Thank you, but we couldn't possibly do that."* Ouch!

CHAPTER 6

HOW TO KEEP CLIENTS AND PROSPECTS ENGAGED BY CREATING NEW AND MEMORABLE EXPERIENCES

People are always seeking relief from the daily grind, the stuck-in-a-rut feeling that is unfortunately pervasive today.

They want to do more, enjoy more, and experience more. But keeping up with their own daily responsibilities of family and business, they just don't have the resource of time or sometimes even the skill set to organize the things they want to do.

Consequently, enjoying new experiences with you that are thoughtful and well-managed builds their portfolio of positive memories about you.

Whether the new experience is social, recreational, or educational, it places them in a different and more relaxed environment with you. The experience and the environment both further reinforce that they are in the right place with the right professional.

And the good news is that what matters is not how much money you spend on a new experience. Rather, it is the thoughtfulness of spending time with them that pays big dividends on both sides of the relationship. They feel confident in you when you spend time with them and demonstrate that you are relationally thinking of them.

You will be blessed by how much your relationships and business will grow through purposeful interaction with others.

After all, "friend raising" precedes fundraising!

These tactics will place you on the path to building a portfolio of great memories, elevated experiences, emotional engagement, and thoughtful relationships.

TACTIC 70: WHAT IS THE BEST TYPE OF EVENT?

I am asked frequently *what is the best type of event to do?*

My reply is always the same: *"I have no idea, but I can assure you that if you ask your clients they will give you real insight and a clear path."*

That is not to say that you should only do one type of event. Instead, it is to remind you that different people respond to and are motivated by different things. Whether you are considering doing educational events, recreational events, or social events, the real magic is in the mix. To get the right mix, the right topics, and the right location, ask your top ten clients what they would enjoy.

Be sure to look at your client experience management (CXM) database for things you captured from your client welcoming checklist and your ongoing interactions that they enjoy.

Some people like golf, some like educational seminars, some just want to be entertained, and some would just enjoy lunch with you. The most important thing about deciding which type of events are best is to consider not the ones you would enjoy the most but rather the ones they will enjoy!

TACTIC 71: WHAT SIZE EVENT IS THE BEST?

Generally speaking, smaller is better so that you can interact with people in a personalized way.

Of course, things like holiday parties or large educational events typically have more people.

However, even with large events, your goal should be to make a personal connection with everyone who attends.

How?

Stop working the room, and instead work the door. I know this flies in the face of common networking ideas and even networking coaching. But remember, this is not about you, it is about you being there for them.

Work the door. Personally greet every single person that comes in with a smile and a positive tone and say, *"So glad you came and delighted to see you. What are you (two) looking forward to the most today/tonight?"*

Note that this is not the standard *"I hope you have a good time."* Instead, it creates a moment of remembrance and positive interaction with every single attendee.

This receiving line that you create at the door will make them feel special and personally welcomed and will allow them to share their thoughts for a moment. After you are certain that everyone has arrived, then work the room.

TACTIC 72: HOW DO YOU ENSURE PEOPLE ARE COMFORTABLE AT A LARGE EDUCATIONAL OR BUSINESS MEETING?

Follow these steps:

Step 1. Choose the right space. A large room beats a too small room every time.

Step 2. Begin well. Have something enjoyable to snack on (not just sliced carrots and celery) and beverages to enjoy. This reduces tension, reduces awkwardness, and creates camaraderie amongst attendees. A story I heard about how Sid Stahl, a first-class mediator, welcomes people to mediation is spot on. He offers warm chocolate chip cookies at the start of each mediation session. Imagine high-powered attorneys relaxing and eating those cookies together before presenting their clients' positions. This is a great way to start an educational seminar or business meeting. People who eat together tend to connect better.

Step 3. Have a name badge for everyone that they fill out with their first names only. Encourage them to place the name badge on their upper right-hand chest so that it is easier for people to read when shaking their hand and speaking with them.

Step 4. Start on time.

Step 5. End on time.

TACTIC 73: BE CREATIVE AND THINK WAY OUTSIDE THE BOX

Whenever I ask others about events they have done, I am always thrilled with their creativity, especially in a world where people want to be part of something fun and exciting.

In addition to asking your top clients and referencing your CXM, let your imagination run free!

A few examples of the types of events you can host include: wine tastings, bourbon tastings, sports game outings, bike safety programs for kids in the community you serve, child ID clinics for elementary school children, progressive course dinners, book readings by a visiting author on tour at the bookstore, a holiday season bible study for a local church group, a picnic to welcome the summer or a party for back to school, a day hike, a spa day, a Mother's Day out luncheon, a cooking class, or dinner by a local chef.

Consider an art and antiques appraisal event (your own *Antiques Roadshow*) in the office or in a gallery. Or a jewelry appraisal night by a high-end jeweler at your office or theirs.

You could have a class on how to select wine in a social setting conducted by a local sommelier for executives and business owners. Or a golf-putting clinic with the club pro on a day when the club is closed for playing.

Or perhaps a car show event, or a boater's water and fire safety event at the yacht club.

These are just a few of the events I have heard about recently. The only limit is your imagination. If money stands in the way, seek a sponsor to partner with you. Where there is a will, there is and always will be a way.

TACTIC 74: KEEP SOCIAL EVENTS SOCIAL

Social events are just that—an opportunity to socialize with others. Do not invite people to an activity billed as a social event and then include a sales talk or a so-called "update."

If the event is going to include *any* type of business activity, real estate market update, product briefing, or service messaging from you or even a sponsor you partner with, make that clear on your invitation.

Why? Because in that case, it is no longer only a social event. It is a *"dinner and market or service update"* event.

These types of events are just fine and are also productive. Just be aware if you bait and switch, even if that is not your intent, it will be perceived as such, and it will seriously erode their trust in you and your relationship with them.

As an example, I heard from a financial team that decided they would not have a sponsor or any product or service messaging at a dinner they were hosting. They wanted a purely social event. They hosted a nice dinner for eight couples, half of whom were clients while the others invited guests of those clients.

One guest told the leader afterward that he was *"pleasantly surprised"* that the leader simply thanked everyone for coming and didn't make a "pitch" about their services. He further commented about how refreshing it was to not attend the *"bait and switch"* dinner event he expected.

Most importantly, that began the start of a relationship which culminated in the guest moving most of his business to the host company in the next six months. Why? They said he was impressed that they were not on the hunt but rather wanted to spend quality time with a few of their clients and a few of their friends.

TACTIC 75: EDUCATE TO MOTIVATE ATTENDEES TO ACTION

You can do educational programs on topics people care about, such as getting your child a scholarship, protecting yourself if you are sued, affording the home of your dreams, affording the retirement you have rightly earned, keys to saving money on taxes, how to lease a car, and so on.

The most valued educational events, however, are those that don't just tell people what they need to do but rather give them the actual steps they can take to get it done.

When you share the "how to," it prompts people to see you for what you really are: the person who knows how to help them get what they want. When attendees see that, they are motivated to reach out and do business with you.

Too many educational events get very low ROI because the information is not actionable, so people dismiss it as not viable or doable. Worse, clients even see it as a thinly veiled sales pitch and not an elevated experience of any kind.

You may also think or have been told that giving out too much "how to" detail can cost you business. But that argument comes from a mindset of scarcity. Give people the direction, the help, and the information they need, and abundance will flood your business—and your life!

TACTIC 76: DON'T HAVE CLIENTS JUST INVITE FRIENDS—INSTEAD, "INVITE UP"

When creating a social, recreational, or educational event that is also used for prospecting, the common practice is to have your clients invite "a friend." The challenge here is that most people have many friends, and unless you're running a dollar store you likely want to be a bit more targeted in your ask.

To help them help you, suggest that they invite someone who potentially has the means to become a client or, at the very least, who will expand your network with the right people.

How can you do that without blatantly saying *"I want qualified people only?"* We all know (even if we hate to admit it) that it is not their job to qualify anyone on your behalf.

The good news is that from your detailed welcoming process, you know most of your clients participate in some organization of some kind. Using that information to guide them on who to invite further solidifies your place with them as a thoughtful, caring person.

Instead of the nebulous *invite a friend*, use this kind language on your written invitation or in your verbal invite: *Please feel welcome to invite another [business owner, professional or executive, club or association member, etc.] like yourself who [collects rare wine, enjoys fine dining, is always interested in the latest ideas, etc.].*

The more specific you are about who to invite, the easier it is for clients to sort through their mental file and invite the right person from their connections. Often it is someone they want to build a stronger relationship with as well, so it becomes a double win for you.

TACTIC 77: GET IN THEIR PHONE AND GET MORE CLIENTS

How can you get back in front of the clients and prospective clients who attend any large educational or social event you organize?

The simple, yet often overlooked answer is to have *everyone* register with both their email address *and* their cell phone number.

Tell them to list their cell number so that if there are any last-minute updates, you can reach them, and they can also reach you.

Then text them your *digital business card* before the event and tell them to save it so they will have your number if they have any questions about the event or if something comes up at the last minute.

When the event is over, you have their number, and they have yours.

This approach also works when you casually meet someone and have a good conversation about what they enjoy, like, or even do. Simply say to them: "*I may have an opportunity for you to [play golf, play tennis, play pickleball, attend a business event, attend an educational event, get some info on that topic]. Let's exchange numbers so we can stay in touch.*"

Make no mistake: if you are not in their phone, you're not really in their network.

TACTIC 78: THE BEST AFTERPARTY THAT WILL IMPROVE YOUR EVENT ROI

Whether you are doing educational briefings, offering social or recreational events, or involved in an activity with an organization, having a personalized post-event strategy is the only way to ensure a return on your time and treasure.

Don't just call or send a note afterwards. You want to stand out from all the others. How? Elevate, elevate, elevate.

Why? The best afterparty is when you reconnect in person with each attendee after the event.

How?

Hand-deliver a memento from the event. It might be a framed photo of the group enjoying the event or cliff notes from the seminar. Or a signed book from the speaker, a cookbook from the chef, or a flight of golf balls or tube of tennis balls from the club where you all played. Or candid photos of the ball game you all attended that you had printed through Shutterfly into a spiral-bound hand-sized album. For clients or prospective clients, this approach reinforces your thoughtfulness and kindness toward them.

For those prospective clients, this approach opens the door to go from meeting them to meeting *with* them. When you hand-deliver the memento, say something like this:

> *Thank you for coming to the [educational briefing, dinner the other evening, etc.]. Here is a small memento for you. What is the one thing you enjoyed the most? (Don't say the generic "did you have a good time?" Listen and learn.) Now that we have spent time together personally, I would like the privilege of introducing myself to you professionally. Let's have breakfast or lunch one day next week and we can have a conversation about your business and mine, and then we can decide*

100 Proven Ways to Acquire and Keep Clients for Life

if we ever need to bring it up again. What is best for you, Tuesday, or Thursday?

Let your imagination run with ways to memorialize the event so that you can get back in front of clients and prospective clients face-to-face to demonstrate your thoughtfulness. One friend of mine, after a great night of steaks for clients and their invited guests, delivers an engraved steak knife to each with their name on it. It is always a *wow!*

TACTIC 79: MAKE THAT UPCOMING SMALL DINNER EVENT MEMORABLE FOR ALL

My wife and I host dinner parties throughout the year, and we have stumbled upon a way to get everyone to have fun *and* build deeper connections. It is always a hit. And yes, this works for small client events too.

Here it is.

First, think about the time of year or the event. There are always holidays, special dates, and events coming up, such as spring and winter breaks, summer vacations, back to school, Valentine's Day, someone's birthday or special anniversary, and so on.

Second, on individual slips of paper (we use Post-it Notes), write out a series of different questions (one on each slip or Post-it) related to the time of year or the event.

Some examples are: *"What is your favorite family (or business) tradition this time of year?" "What is the one gift you always wanted but never got?" "What is the most random last-minute gift you ever bought?"*

Have enough slips for everyone at the table and be sure not to repeat a question to ensure that everyone has their own unique one.

It is important to write the questions on a slip of paper so people can think about their answer. Otherwise, just verbalizing a question puts people on the spot and creates tension instead of tremendous fun.

Third, just after everyone has put a good dent in their entrée, pass a bowl with the slips of paper in them, and have each person blindly draw one slip.

Then, go around the table one at a time and have each person read their question aloud and answer it. You won't believe the stories, the laughter, and the "*let me tell you what I did*" additions.

Helping people connect with others is fun, memorable, and relational.

My wife and I just smile when people say, "*You two are the best hosts; we have so much fun.*" We are grateful, but all we did was write out a few questions and then sit back and enjoy watching people having a fun time relating to each other and to us. You will too. It is truly a path to a portfolio of memories.

TACTIC 80: THE POWER OF THE NON-BUSINESS BREAKFAST OR LUNCH

My good friend and spiritual dad, Ken Clary, who I mentioned in my acknowledgments, is ninety-three years old at this writing. He was recognized for more than sixty years as the number-one manufacturer's representative for industrial water heaters and boilers in the country.

Ken said he knew from his first sales call right out of college that relationships would be the key to getting his heaters specified on a job by an engineer.

As a result, nearly every day of the week for six decades(!), he took an engineer to breakfast and another to lunch.

As a rainmaker who sold thousands of commercial heaters, he focused on building a valued relationship with each person because, as he said, *"They are not just engineers or clients; they are also my friends."* He epitomizes my point earlier that friend raising precedes fundraising.

To this day, even in his "retirement," he has breakfast and lunch several days a week with these "friends." There is a great lesson here for all who want to create a sustainable business. Build rock-solid relationships by taking a personal interest in each of your clients and treating them as people. When people break bread together, a stronger relationship is on the menu.

TACTIC 81: HELP OTHERS TO GET THE CONVERSATION OR Q&A STARTED

Social events and large educational and business meetings can be stressful for many people.

Socially, they might not be sure how to start a conversation without using the default, *"So, what do you do?"*

In educational and business meetings, many are reticent to speak in public to ask a question, or they are afraid they will *"sound dumb."*

Here is how *you* can solve both problems.

The Social Event

If you are at a social event, you can engage people very graciously and be seen as approachable and real.

Skip the default *"Hi, nice to meet you…so, what do you do?"*

Instead, as I mentioned in a previous chapter, say *"nice to see you"* when introduced to someone, and then immediately ask them *"how long have you known…and how did you meet?"* or *"how long have you been a member here at…and what prompted you to join?"* Or *"when did you first get interested in…?"*

They will love you for providing them with an opening to start a conversation. Always remember to ask them something that gives them an opportunity to *tell a bit of their story.*

It creates an engaging memorable conversation.

The Educational Event

In an educational session or large business meeting you are hosting, a fun and easy solution I use all the time to break the tension around asking a question is this: "*Okay, this is your time to ask any questions you may have… so, who would like to go second, because I know nobody wants to go first?*"

The audience's laughter breaks the tension, and then there is usually a competition over who can get their hand up fastest for me to call on them.

Implementing these simple shifts doesn't mean you have to be the life of the party. Just help people engage, and it will get you miles of goodwill and a bank of relational capital from clients, who will appreciate how nice and thoughtful you are.

TACTIC 82: TIPS FOR BEING CONFIDENTLY CONVERSATIONAL AND ENGAGING

All of us at one time or another feel less than confident about our social skills. Yet good social skills are essential to building a successful business and meaningful relationships. One way to improve and build your confidence is to assess where you see yourself and how you will improve. Then when you do events of any kind, you can focus on the attendees having a great time because you have already determined how you will be more socially engaging and conversational with everyone.

Here Are a Few Ways You Can Do This

1. Come into every social conversation with a "positive attitude of gratitude."

It really helps to start any introduction, conversation, or formal meeting with a smile and an attitude of positive gratitude. People today have a great deal going on in their lives. Your cheerful outlook that exudes gratitude is a true bright light in their day and will make meeting you and meeting with you memorable. Also, choosing gratitude will benefit you as it replaces anxious responses. It calms you down and rewires your thought process. You will find yourself focused more on them and less on yourself.

2. Keep eye contact and avoid distractions.

As I mentioned in a previous chapter, be sure to keep eye contact and avoid distractions when you are engaged in even a brief conversation. When you keep eye contact, people feel like they are the only person in the room.

3. Use your voice for emphasis and sustaining interest.

Use your voice to make sure you are perceived as conversational by "landing" your points appropriately, as opposed to mumbling or trailing off. This is especially important to give the person with whom you are speaking confidence in what you are saying.

4. Prepare in advance.

I know a professional who attended a fundraiser for a new football stadium for the local college in his hometown. He wasn't an alumnus of that college and didn't follow the team. However, one of his clients had invited him, and it was a great opportunity to meet his client's friends. Prior to the event, he thought of some questions to ask so he would feel comfortable and confident once he arrived:

> *What do you think of the new stadium plans?*
> *Has there been any pushback from surrounding neighborhoods?*
> *How do you like the new class of players coming in?*
> *How do you like the team's chances next year?*
> *How long have you been going to games here?*

The response was, as he said, *"very gratifying."* People engaged with him, and in just a few minutes he felt like he was part of that group, and he made several new friends.

TACTIC 83: EVERY EVENT NEEDS A PRE-, DURING-, AND POST-EVENT STRATEGY

If you are doing a large client appreciation event, a holiday party, or an educational seminar, it is essential that you look at the event from three angles—the pre-event stage, the during-event stage, and the post-event stage.

The same also applies to smaller events, including breakfast, lunch, or dinner with clients or prospective clients.

This three-tiered vantage point will ensure that your key objectives will be met at each phase and that the event will be a strategic and relational success.

For large events, craft a detailed checklist in a pre/during/post format. List everything: type of room, menu tastings, educational content, entertainment, seating type, pad and pens for educational note taking by attendees, and so on. This approach will help you think strategically and tactically about how you can elevate the attendee experience. It will also help maximize the return on your investment of your time and treasure.

I have provided a sample Pre-, During-, and Post-Large-Event Checklist at the end of this tactic for you to reference. (You can download this tool as a Word Document at RichardWeylman.com under the Resource Tab.)

If the event you're planning seems a bit overwhelming, hire a professional meeting planner. It is money well spent and will save you much anxiety, to say nothing of the added monetary and reputational costs of any mistakes. Meeting Professionals International (MPI, mpi.org) is a reliable source of planners and other meeting professionals.

For smaller events such as breakfast or lunch with a client or prospective client, while a detailed formal checklist may not be needed, you still must think strategically and tactically if you want to deepen your relationship and opportunities with your guest(s).

Here is how your checklist should be organized:

1. The pre-event plan should clearly state the location, day, time, and attendees.

2. The during-event plan for the day of the event should include the seating area and arrangement. If there is a view, be sure guests can see it. Your credit or debit card should be given for payment before guests arrive, and the group picture location should be chosen if it is part of your post-event plan.

3. The post-event plan should include a scheduled date on your calendar to hand-deliver the group picture or other memento, a tentative date for a next business steps meeting, and/or the date of the social or recreational event to which you will invite the attendees.

Sample Pre-, During-, and Post-Large-Event Checklists

Pre-Event: Get organized

Pre-Event Action Items	Who?	When?	Results
Establish Success Indicators— Goals should be for number of referred leads, appointments, and sales			
Choose location and date			
Define best profile for audience			
Identify clients who fit best profile (assume guest)			
Identify prospects who will be invited			
Determine if sponsors or charity will be involved			
Confirm details of formal contract (if necessary)			
Determine scope of menu			
Estimate cost per person			
Book A/V professional and/or photographer			
Develop the agenda and other aspects of event (e.g., raffle or benefit for charity)			

Coordinate donations/ commitments from sponsors; obtain logos for invitation			
Get client/prospect lists from sponsors			
If other speakers or a panel are used, have conversation to determine topics and relay specific expectations			
Begin to formulate educational presentation material if that is the purpose or a part of the event			
Send sample agenda and confirmation letters to sponsors			
Send educational materials to compliance for approval if needed			
Get biographies of speakers			
Get three quotes for invitation design			
Ensure that all clients and prospects are in CXM database; set up separate file for seminar mailing			
Email or fax "Save the Date" flyer			
Order formal invitations and reply cards			
Mail invitations with reply card			
Enter confirmed registrations in database with cell numbers			

Call all registrants to confirm			
Call all confirmed non-attendees to convey regrets and promise follow-up materials			
Call all non-responders to convert to registrants			
Make onsite visit to map out event flow; ensure adequate A/V equipment (e.g., microphones); test to ensure success			
Obtain any handout materials from sponsors in advance			
Create educational packages including event evaluation sheet			
Create name tags for all registered guests			
Write press release and submit to local press			
Order any A/V equipment that may be necessary (e.g., big screen or lavaliere microphone)			
Order pencils and pads			
Determine if any special seating arrangements are advisable for ease of networking			
Review Post-Event activities and set aside time in calendar			

Engage a writer to summarize highlights of event for post-event; give them as much information in advance to avoid delays after the event for PR release			
Create signs (e.g., "Welcome from our team and sponsors," "Please turn off cell phones")			
Obtain prices for post-event hand-delivered gift or memento			
Run through presentation with all speakers			
Additional notes:			

During Event—Be sure everything runs smoothly

During-Event Action Items	Who?	When?	Results
Our sales and service professionals are positioned for networking only			
We have defined success and have those indicators in mind (e.g., expecting specific introductions and scheduling of next-step appointments)			
Greet attendees at door and engage them			
For onsite registration, be sure it is organized so that no one waits more than five minutes			
Arrange the room to look full, with food in central area to keep people mingling in the middle			
Check A/V and lighting again			
Place educational packages, pencils, and pads at each table; centerpieces as appropriate			
Give sponsors favorable exposure; if tables are set up for giveaways, ensure they are in full view and well-appointed			
Ensure written speeches and presentation materials are at the ready			
Ensure the event starts on time			
Relay any housekeeping comments at the start			

Additional notes:			

Post-Event: The "afterparty"

Post-Event Action Items	Who?	When?	Results
Send thank-you notes to all sponsors and speakers (as appropriate)			
Develop photos, edit video or audio			
Post event photos online			
Call every attendee and non-attendee			
Make appointments to drop off memento from the event (photo, book, etc.)			
Track appointments made in CXM database			
Consider post-event press release			
Incorporate all attendees and non-attendees into ongoing CXM cultivation system			
Send attendee thank-you letters or emails after hand-delivering the memento			
When hand-delivering the memento, be sure to use the transition language in Tactic 78 here to go from meeting people to meeting with people			

Additional notes:

CHAPTER 7

HOW TO BE SURE CLIENTS AND PROSPECTS ALWAYS KNOW YOU VALUE THEM AND THEIR RELATIONSHIP WITH YOU

My wife used a first-time buyer coupon to purchase some products online and save 20 percent on her order. She loved the products and decided to reorder. When she logged in there was no coupon for returning customers. She called the company and asked if they had a coupon or code for repeat customers.

The CSR said, *"Oh no, we don't do that."* Great. No reward for loyalty.

This scenario is similar to the attention prospects are given when people are attempting to gain their business. Or the attention new clients are given during the welcoming process. Just like a new customer coupon, they both get rewarded with special and usually undivided attention.

But what happens after they become a "client?" Well, for some, if they are a big enough client, they may receive some regular attention.

But for most, there is no reward. No consistently elevated experiences, no regularly scheduled or personalized attention or communication. Sure, they get their statements from the firm, a newsletter, and the occasional review, but that pales in comparison to their previous experience of undivided attention as a new client.

Is it any wonder, then, that people take their business somewhere else?

Unfortunately, because so many businesses and professionals do not realize or are unaware of the lifetime value of each client, many opportunities are lost because of the lack of ongoing communication and cultivation.

Regardless of the business you are in, having a sustainable relationship with your clients requires thoughtful, proactive, regular communication and ongoing personalized cultivation. This tells them that you are always thinking of them and that you value their relationship with you.

Without ongoing thoughtful communication and personalized cultivation that ensures top-of-mind awareness, people are drawn to other suppliers, who are of course constantly working hard to get your clients' attention.

Or they use the internet and social media to find the answers they seek. There, they are exposed to both conflicting viewpoints and competitive options.

A lack of proactive, meaningful communication is consistently mentioned as one of the primary reasons many clients leave.

Clients also become frustrated or disenchanted, or feel taken for granted, when the only time they hear from you is when it is time to buy something, change something, or review something.

You may be good at delivering and servicing your products and services, but other businesses and their professionals are too.

Yes, people do business where they are invited and feel emotionally and economically secure. However, they only stay when they feel valued and appreciated.

If you want to grow and retain your business, be mindful that relationships, just like a garden, need to be fertilized and watered regularly. My example of Chewy in the introduction is just one example of how to cultivate relationships and build advocacy with the people you serve.

Another example of how to value and appreciate clients was demonstrated by a financial advisor I met. He sends out his client's quarterly financial statements, but he always makes a comment on a specific item in the report to initiate questions relative to his client's goals. It would be far easier for him to ask his assistant or the firm to generate and send the reports out, but then he wouldn't be able to provide the personal commentary that has become his hallmark.

The tactics that follow will put you on the path that says to clients, *"Welcome home. We value you and our relationship with you."* Your advocacy for them will translate into their loyalty and their advocacy for you.

TACTIC 84: WHEN TRAGEDY STRIKES OR BAD THINGS HAPPEN, DON'T JUST SAY SOMETHING—DO SOMETHING!

A dear friend of mine had a thirty-two-year-old grandson who was murdered. The outpouring of condolences was simply remarkable. More than seven hundred people attended his funeral.

Several days later, my friend said, "*So many kept saying, 'If there is anything I can do for you, let me know,' but very few actually did anything. But for those that did something without being asked, we will never forget and will always be grateful.*"

When tragedy of any kind strikes, the people involved are reeling and struggling to think about anything else. While saying "*If there is anything I can do for you, let me know*" is very kind, it is the actions *taken* on their behalf that are never forgotten.

This knowledge made me think about the actions that people took for that family that *did* make a difference. A big difference!

I thought of the friend who called the mother who had just lost her son and said, "*I will host a remembrance brunch for him at my club,*" then did just that.

Or the advisor who knew that many would gather at the family home and, without being asked, delivered several cases of water and boxes of snacks to the home.

Or the neighbor who fed the family dog every day and night for an entire week to give the family more time to grieve.

When tragedy or a major illness strikes a client, or the family of a close friend, always be proactive:

- *"What do you have at the dry cleaner that I can pick up?"*
- *"I am going to get the car washed for you."*
- *"I am going to the store to pick up anything you need."*
- *"What night may I bring dinner over for you?"*

Even if you are hundreds of miles away, there is still much you can do. For example, you can order footlong subs or pizzas via a food delivery app.

The actions you take on behalf of others are remembered long after even your kindest spoken words are forgotten.

As I am writing this chapter, Claudia Waterloo, a successful financial advisor, has just shared a wonderful story and process with me about her mother's passing.

It is a process every one of you, regardless of industry or role in it, should note and inform your clients and family about in the event of a loved one's death.

While Claudia took care of the legal and financial matters, one brother snapped pictures of everything in her mother's place, including the insides of cabinets.

Another brother then numbered and captioned over two hundred photos, loaded them to a shared drive, and built a spreadsheet.

They then had a Zoom giveaway of her possessions with all eleven family members across five states. Each went in order, making their selections in turn. Over four hours and seventeen rounds, hundreds of items were chosen. As Claudia remembers, "It was actually great fun and a marvelous use of technology!"

Death of a loved one is always difficult, indeed heartbreaking. Often, the distribution of the departed's possessions puts additional stress and strain on families and their relationships.

The innovative process that Claudia's family used was "great fun"—something that is sorely needed in times of grief.

The important point here is: If you become aware of any tragedy, accident, or bad news your client is experiencing, don't just say something—do something.

It doesn't have to be a grand gesture, but it should be a personal gesture: a handwritten note if a pet passes away, flowers in a vase, or a batch of homemade cookies.

TACTIC 85: MASSAGE YOUR SOCIAL MEDIA MESSAGING SO THAT PEOPLE RELATE TO IT

Tomes have been written by others about using social media to promote your product, your service, or even yourself.

Yet little has been mentioned about using it to communicate and cultivate positive relationships.

We know from our research and experience that one proven way to use social media to build and cultivate relationships is to tell relatable real-life stories with actionable insight.

People today are jaded, divided, cynical, and just plain sick and tired of all the memes and mindless hyped promotion.

What people want is authenticity and an emotional connection.

What exactly does authenticity mean when it comes to messaging and posting?

It means that people want to better understand not only who you are but whether you can actually relate to them and their own situations.

They want to feel the message is specifically created *for* them.

So many professionals and firms are focused on being "professional" that their authenticity and ability to have an emotional connection isn't visible. If you want to stand out, it is important that you write and talk about the human side of your business in your posts, emails, and presentations.

For example, you could address:

- The difficulties people encounter buying a luxury item, preparing for retirement, buying a home, setting up a trust, filing their taxes, choosing a college, and so on. Then, you want to tell them how those issues can be or have been solved.

- Setbacks that you have actually seen when people focus only on pricing and don't ever evaluate the added value of a relationship with a company and a professional. Then provide guidance on how to assess real, personal, relational value.

- Moments of clarity that you or a client achieved and how those moments affected you and them, both then and now going forward.

- How important it was in the case of a tragedy or natural disaster for those who were affected to be prepared and what they did.

Telling relatable stories and giving actionable insights, whether in writing or via two-minute videos, continually refreshes your passion and purpose.

Tell your stories and theirs. People will relate to you, engage with you, and stay with you.

Just be mindful that people have very short attention spans, so be brief, be brilliant, be bold, and be gone!

To see examples, visit (feel welcome to subscribe to) my YouTube channel: www.youtube.com/@RichardWeylman.

TACTIC 86: AVOID SENDING OR POSTING ANYTHING GENERIC ANYWHERE

The watchwords for any communication sent or posted are to be relevant, meaningful, and mindful of the recipients.

Segment your CXM so that when you proactively send out information, your newsletter, or a link to your blog or social media posting, it communicates "we know you and are thinking of you." Sending a retiree a newsletter or a posting that is only about "How to write a resume and get hired" is of questionable value for that person, to say the least.

No matter what you offer the marketplace, it is important that the reader realizes that you know them and care enough about them to inform them on topics that are relevant and meaningful.

In addition, in the many newsletters, social media postings, and blog content I have reviewed for clients, too often I find that the content is promotional and transactional. It is all about convincing people to buy something more. It is messaging that focuses just on your "Ps"—your products, processes, performance, platforms, or people. Instead, set yourself apart and send positive, powerful, productive market-segmented information that educates people on things they wish to accomplish and how you are there to help them.

Doing so will cultivate your relationship with them, and they will want to know more about the topic or your product or service, and in the end, they will do more business with you.

TACTIC 87: CALL WITH THE INTENT TO REFERENCE WHAT THEY HAVE SHARED PREVIOUSLY

People will tell you about many things through the course of your relationships. They will share with you what their children are doing, where they are going on vacation, who has been ill, and much more.

This emotional and relational connection that they make with you is wonderful. They tell you things that are personal to them and the details about their lives because they trust you and relate to you. They want you to know them and know about them, their families, their situations. It is thus vital that when they share even the smallest detail that you capture that detail in your CXM. Why? Because when you speak to them again, you will be able to reference what they said and ask them for an update.

I have a client in West Virginia who mentioned to me that his daughter Jennifer was trying out for the cheerleading squad the next day. She had been practicing day and night for weeks. When I spoke with him two months later, I asked, *"How did Jennifer do with the cheerleading squad tryouts?"* He was surprised I had remembered (thank you, CXM!). Then he spent several minutes telling me all about how she had made the squad and how proud he was of her. Demonstrating an interest in the life events of others weaves you into their life fabric.

TACTIC 88: GIVE TO GIVE AGAIN AND SUPPORT THEIR COMMUNITY

People have become extremely interested in the ways that their professional is involved in and contributes to their community.

What they care about is not just the company's contribution or involvement but the actual professional with whom they do business.

People want to do business with those professionals who are giving back and are demonstrating their own desire to make a difference. Professionals who show they are doing good (not boasting but demonstrating) while also making money will gain much respect and will be seen as thoughtful, caring, kind, and empathetic individuals.

A recent study of 530 executives by Oomiji Technology found that 92 percent believe supporting and helping local residential and business communities is a demonstrable point of distinction.

However, to be truly distinct, realize that your mindset should be "you give to be able to give again," rather than "you give to get," which is often seen as non-authentic and only manipulative.

A great example is JoyRide Cars, founded in Dayton, Ohio, by Blair Cornell, a financial advisor with a special needs child and a heart for giving to give again.

JoyRide Cars is a car club exclusively for kids with special needs. Twice per year, dozens of exotic car owners gather at large parking lots and give the kids rides in their cars through a pylon-marked course. The community has responded, and JoyRide Cars has been recognized by local leaders and the media for the positive impact on the community and the nearly 1,200 people that now attend their gatherings.

What does Blair receive from his efforts? The opportunity to be a continual blessing to many special needs kids and their families.

As a JoyRide parent said, *"If you want to see unfiltered happiness, you should see the kids' faces when they climb out of the cars."* That is better than any financial reward one could receive.

There are many ways you can be involved in your community, so don't overthink it. Choose something you are passionate about and would enjoy doing and supporting. It may be supporting a local youth baseball team, participating in a walk for a serious illness to raise funds, or helping children manage a lemonade stand. My young neighbors did the last activity on that list with their children just last Saturday morning and raised $1,200 for a childhood cancer cure. *Wow!*

When possible, support the things and causes your clients are passionate about *if*, and only if, you are also passionate about that same cause. And focus your attention and efforts to support what that cause does, not just how much you give.

TACTIC 89: RECOGNIZE PEOPLE INSIDE AND OUTSIDE YOUR MARKET

There was a story that recently went viral about a Kentucky coal miner named Michael McGuire who went straight from work, still wearing his work clothes, to join his wife and three-year-old son at a University of Kentucky basketball game. It was his son's first game, and he had promised to be there, so there he sat, covered in coal dust, but keeping his promise.

The head coach of the team heard the story and decided to do something special for this coal miner dad who mirrored his family values. He shared the photo with his Twitter followers to locate the McGuire family, then invited them as his guests to another game of their choice. The coach hosted the family as VIPs with courtside seats, and Michael even played the part of the special guest "Y" in Kentucky when it was spelled out by the cheer team.

Who is the unrecognized person or client you know in the market you are targeting and working? Who has done so much for so many that what they did should be recognized? There are many kinds of Halls of Fame. Maybe you should start one for the people in your market. A local vocational teacher, or first responder, or caregiver Hall of Fame, or special needs Parent of the Year. You get the idea. The more you focus on others, the more gratifying your work becomes for you. When people see your passion and gratitude, it makes them feel delighted that they are doing business with you.

TACTIC 90: INCREASE YOUR VISIBILITY AND THUS YOUR VIABILITY

People today are actively networking like never before with those with similar interests, in social clubs, charitable societies, business organizations, and more—from golf, yacht, and pickleball clubs to professional associations and even purpose-driven nonprofits. The good news is that when you make the effort to become part of their network, it places you in a unique position to elevate and cultivate your relationship with them and their peers. When you are part of their network, they see you contributing in a different setting and supporting things that are important to them.

This makes them feel confident that you know and understand them and that your values are congruent with their own.

People also feel more confident that you can help them if you are in "their network." As part of their network, you can ask to be a part of their podcast, partner with them on social activities, participate in events and meetings and even serve on committees. By getting involved in their network, you will be seen as a partner in the things that interest them. One of the greatest accomplishments you can achieve is to be seen by clients as a thoughtful, kind, caring, and empathetic member of their personal network.

TACTIC 91: SOMETIMES YOU MAY HAVE TO CREATE YOUR OWN NETWORK

I have a friend who wanted to meet more people in her neighborhood. She started a ladies' tennis league for her neighbors and hired a pro for the first two hours to get it going. It has gone so well that she has added to the offering by encouraging her neighbors to try pickleball. She again made it easy to participate by bringing in a woman well known in the neighborhood to teach a lesson. There were seven new players on the first night. She is expanding her network and making new friends every week. She is doing all this to build up her community.

You could do the same thing with a core group of clients who will invite others to participate. Case in point: a client wanted to create a forum for executives in his targeted industry. He talked to four of his clients who all agreed to participate and invite other executives to the first meeting. The first meeting was breakfast, and the topic—"How to Navigate Industry Regulations," presented by a noted attorney—was a big draw, with fourteen CEOs in attendance. Today, six years later, the forum every other month averages more than forty-five CEOs. Our client has captured the business of nearly every CEO in that regional marketplace because he created a network for them, and they have come to know him and see him as their financial resource.

TACTIC 92: SEND SPECIAL NOTES ON THEIR SPECIAL DAYS

We all have and enjoy special days. They are usually times of celebration and often include reflection and a feeling of gratitude.

Of course, there are the birthdays and traditional holidays that most of us are aware of, and that various people celebrate as special.

It is common to send well wishes on a client's birthday or a client's religious holiday, such as Hanukkah, Diwali, Eid, Kwanzaa, or Christmas.

However, most of them will get cards or a message from others on these days. So, while it is good to send a special note, be mindful that after yours is read it is likely to be placed in the stack with the others. Thus, it is important to really focus on and do what others don't.

Here are some ideas:

- Send a special note on their business or employment anniversary. When I was in the Rolls-Royce business, I always asked my clients *"What month did you start your business?"* Every year, I would send them a card congratulating them on another successful year in business. It was amazing how many thank-you calls I received and how many business conversations resulted.

- Send a note on their first purchase anniversary. It amazes me that Five-O Donut Co, the original home of "arrestingly good donuts" next to the police station in Sarasota, Florida, is way ahead of most on this. Every year on August 4, I get a text from them saying *"Congratulations on your loyalty anniversary. Here is five dollars off your next Five-O Donut."* Similarly, the guy who sold me my first luxury car sent me a "thank you for your business" note every year on my first purchase anniversary until I moved several states away out of his authorized delivery zone. I bought two more luxury cars from him in four years before moving.

Unfortunately, when most people buy a home, make an investment, buy a policy, pay their first bill for a service, get their air conditioning fixed, or get their car repaired, they never hear from that professional or company again. Opportunity lost. This is especially unfortunate when technology makes it so easy to keep in touch.

Make downloading client purchase anniversaries or business start dates a part of your CXM monthly action items. Then send a handwritten note every year on that very special day.

To make it easy for you and memorable for them, keep a box of note cards and stamps on hand. A friend of mine is an avid fisherwoman and does a lot of work with members of her local fishing club that has a membership of eight hundred. Her notecards are prints of a striped bass that have become so collectible she has seen them framed in her client's offices.

Your notes will also be remembered and appreciated.

TACTIC 93: RECOGNIZE THEM ON THEIR NATIONALLY CELEBRATED OCCUPATIONAL, PROFESSIONAL, AND/OR SPECIAL INTEREST DAYS

Another powerful way to cultivate clients and prospective clients is to recognize their work and their interests. This not only strengthens your relationship with them but also helps them feel confident that you know them and that they are in the right place with the right professional. Every day of the year is designated for multiple occupations, professions, and organizations. To get you started, as of this writing, you can find national day calendars at:

- *www.nationaldaycalendar.com*
- *www.nationaltoday.com*

You can order greeting cards for these special appreciation days at:

- *www.greetingcarduniverse.com*

And yes, there is a day for nearly everybody and everything. Such as:

- *Dentist Appreciation Day*
- *Grandparent Appreciation Day*
- *International Firefighters Day*
- *Teacher Appreciation Day*
- *National Caregivers' Day*
- *World Plumbing Day*
- *National Daughters' Day*
- *National Sons' Day*
- *Hot and Spicy Food Day*
- *…and hundreds more!*

TACTIC 94: WHEN THE OCCASION IS RIGHT, SEND A GIFT

Not every occasion warrants a gift, but special days certainly do. I am not talking about Thanksgiving turkey or pumpkin pie, although they are often welcomed and appreciated. Rather, consider a gift for a milestone birthday or wedding anniversary.

Other possibilities include graduation or recovery from a severe illness or injury. You decide what is best based upon your relationship with them.

One friend of mine knew one of her best NYC clients was celebrating their thirtieth wedding anniversary in Arizona at a luxury resort. They were excited about the trip and the opportunity to have dinner at the legendary restaurant there on their anniversary.

My friend called the resort ahead of time, and when the time came for the couple to pay for their dinner, they received a card instead: *"Happy Anniversary! I love having you both as clients and friends."* Now, before you decide that you could never spend that much, remember it really is the thought that counts.

For a special birthday or anniversary, go to bakemeawish.com and order one of their delicious cakes. They deliver nationwide.

If the kids were accepted to the school they always longed for or the new pet has arrived, go to zazzle.com for personalized gifts.

If a special family reunion is coming up, have family surname ball caps made for everyone.

If someone has a cancer diagnosis and is receiving treatments, send them a plush blue blanket to keep them warm during their treatments.

TACTIC 95: WHEN GIFTING, THINK LOCATION, LOCATION, LOCATION

On those special occasions when you will send a physical gift and not just a card, be sure to send it to your client's place of work.

Why? If it is a cake, a pie, nuts, or anything else delicious, it will likely end up in the breakroom to be shared with others.

There is no substitute for your client sharing your gifts with others. When they are asked *"Where did this come from and what is the occasion?"* they get to talk about how thoughtful you are and what a great experience they have as your client. That alone makes you a standout in this world.

The same holds true when you gift donuts to the nurse's station, the first responder's lounge, the delivery depot, the auto dealership, the boat yard, the yacht club, or any other group you want to cultivate.

TACTIC 96: USE VIDEO TO MAKE A MEMORABLE IMPACT

In this age of advanced technology, there are many ways to communicate and cultivate your clients and prospective clients. One of the most effective ways is to use personalized video—not a high-cost big production video, but a cell phone video (which is great in most models)—to message a client or a group of clients.

One of our clients brilliantly demonstrated the impact a personal video can have. When Mother's Day rolled around, they decided not to send cards this year. Instead, they chose to record a thirty-second Mother's Day video message on their phone and send it to each client.

The simple message went something like this: *"Thank you for the difference you are making in the lives of your family and in the community. Happy Mother's Day to all our mothers and to all your mothers."*

That message resonated so much that it was shared many times on social media by recipients.

You can do the same thing by just taking a moment and asking yourself: *If they were here in front of me, what would I say to them?* Then say it into your phone's camera, and you now have a personalized message to send.

TACTIC 97: I AM ON HOME PLATE, AND YOU'RE OUT!

Never call a client or prospective client just to *"touch base."* What does *that* mean?

I did that years ago with a prospective client, and he said, *"Really? I am on home plate, and you're out"* and hung up. I never used the phrase after that.

I encourage you to never use it either. Forward progress in this hard-to-reach world requires purposeful communications. Instead, call them to *"see how you are," "give you an update," "check on your business,"* or *"provide you some additional thoughts and steps."*

When you take a personal interest in them, you engage them emotionally and motivate them to do more with you, and it increases their advocacy for your work.

TACTIC 98: STRUCTURED COMMUNICATION IS A WIN FOR EVERYONE

In this age of interactive and communicative technology, it is remarkable that so many people feel taken for granted.

This feeling is often a direct result of a lack of structured personal communication from their chosen professional. Doctors, dentists, pharmacies, and other health providers have structured contact, and it pays off with client loyalty.

Recent studies by Pew Research indicate that up to 70 percent of top clients leave a professional due to a lack of structured communications.

Many excuses are offered as to why communications cannot be made on a scheduled, structured, and regular basis. Most often, the excuse is *"We are so busy we don't have time to have anything that structured."*

While you may believe that, be aware that your client will never accept busyness as a reason for poor communications.

If you are unsure of how often to communicate, ask your clients how often they would like to hear from you. If necessary, you can say: *"We have several ways to communicate. We have plan A, where I will call you once each quarter, and we have plan B, where I will call you every six months. Which do you prefer?"*

TACTIC 99: USE TECHNOLOGY AND KEEP PEOPLE UP TO SPEED

With all the incredible technologies available today, you should use your skills and abilities on all communication platforms that fit your market and product.

Gone are the days when running an ad was the most preferred way to reach new people or PR was the only way to inform people. Do those approaches still work? Yes, but there are many other ways to communicate with and cultivate your clients and prospective clients.

Today, you can inform your clients and reach new people at the same time using personal video messages straight to their inbox, as I mentioned in a previous tactic. You can use blog posts, e-zines, newsletters, social media posts, informative articles on topics of interest, Instagram, Facebook, or a purpose-driven app. The sky is the limit.

However, be mindful: while the magic is in the mix of tools you use, limit yourself to two to three and really be brilliant with those. Otherwise, mediocrity will reign as you will be spread far too thin.

And be mindful again that your goal is to be brief, be brilliant, be bold, and be gone!

TACTIC 100: CRAFT A COMMUNICATION AND CULTIVATION CALENDAR

There is no substitute for being organized so that you can communicate with and cultivate your clients.

An example of how to keep yourself organized is the incredible "Annual Client Cultivation and Marketing Calendar" below from my friend and colleague Tiffany A. Markarian, founder and owner of Advantus Marketing, LLC, an award-winning marketing strategist and management consulting firm.

Here, she details seasonal activities a financial professional can use to cultivate their clients and prospects. You can and should craft a similar type of calendar for your client contacts, so no opportunities are lost. (You can download this tool as a Word Document at RichardWeylman.com under the Resource Tab.)

Annual Marketing, Social Media, & Client Cultivation Calendar

January	February
Happy New Year Cards	Black History Month
National Law Enforcement Appreciation Day	World Cancer Day
	National Pizza Day
Martin Luther King, Jr. Day	International Day of Women/Girls in Science
Hot and Spicy Food Day	
Chinese New Year (changes annually)	Valentine's Day
	International Childhood Cancer Day
	National Caregivers' Day

Suggested Financial Communications	Suggested Financial Communications
• *Letter to clients on Practice Announcements (i.e., new staff, new technology, new DBA)* • *Letter to clients to reach out for any investment or insurance tax documents needed*	• *Send cards or call widow/ widower clients to wish them a Happy Valentine's Day* • *Investment education campaigns* • *Announce your firm's/team's philanthropic efforts and thank your clients for helping make the contributions possible*

March	April
Mardi Gras	World Autism Awareness Day
World Wildlife Day	International Children's Book Day
Employee Appreciation Day	National Dental Hygienists' Week
National Dentists' Day	Passover
International Women's Day	World Health Day
World Plumbing Day	Earth Day
Set Clocks Ahead	Administrative Professionals' Day (Take your assistants to lunch or send flowers/gift cards.)
World Down Syndrome Day	
National Doctors' Day	
Transgender Day of Visibility	
Suggested Financial Communications	**Suggested Financial Communications**
• *Client Educational Seminar (i.e., Healthcare and Medicare in Retirement/Social Security)*	• *CPA "Take a Break" Coffee Gift Cards—send your CPAs/Enrolled Agents well wishes in the home stretch of tax season and tell them to enjoy a coffee break on you*

May	June
Asian American and Pacific Islander Heritage Month	National Donut Day
National Teachers' Day	World Oceans Day
International Firefighters' Day	International Sushi Day
Cinco de Mayo	Juneteenth
National Nurses' Day	National Insurance Awareness Day
National Dog Rescue Day	Take Your Dog to Work Day
Memorial Day	
World Multiple Sclerosis Day	
Suggested Financial Communications	**Suggested Financial Communications**
• *Disability Insurance Awareness Month*	• *College Education Funding Campaigns* • *Business Succession Planning Campaigns*

July	August
International Joke Day	National Chocolate Chip Cookie Day
Canada Day	International Cat Day
Independence Day (**Send "A" Clients Apple Pies!**)	International Day of Indigenous People
World Chocolate Day	National Aviation Day
National Ice Cream Day	International Dog Day
International Day of Friendship	
Suggested Financial Communications • *Q2 market updates/ investment briefings*	**Suggested Financial Communications** • *Prep for September Life Insurance Awareness Month*

September	October
World Beard Day	International Coffee Day
International Bacon Day	National Cinnamon Roll Day
Labor Day	National Taco Day
Grandparents' Day	National Coaches' Day
Hispanic Heritage Month (Ends October 15)	Indigenous Peoples' Day (United States)
International Country Music Day	National Coming Out Day (LGBTQIA+)
World Alzheimer's Day	National Bosses' Day
World Gratitude Day	World Pasta Day
Yom Kippur	Halloween
National Daughters' Day	
National Sons' Day	
Suggested Financial Communications	**Suggested Financial Communications**
• *Life Insurance Awareness Month* • *Term Conversion Campaigns* • *Beneficiary Audit Reminder Letters*	• *Investor Education Month Campaigns* • *National Estate Planning Month Campaigns* • *Family "Financial Fire Drill" Campaigns* • *Roth IRA/IRA/SEP Contribution Reminders*

November	December
Set Clocks Back (Daylight Savings Time Ends)	United Nation's International Day of Persons with Disabilities
Veterans' Day	Hanukkah
World Diabetes Day	National Hot Cocoa Day
National Adoption Day	Christmas Eve
	Christmas
	Kwanzaa
	New Year's Eve
Suggested Financial Communications • *Long-Term Care (LTC) Awareness Month Campaigns* • *LTC Educational Letters* • *LTC Hybrid Solutions Campaigns*	**Prepare Holiday Cards** **Prepare New Year's Celebration Cards**

The calendar and ideas herein, compiled by Advantus Marketing, LLC, are meant for educational purposes only and are not intended to replace the need for legal, regulatory, tax, human resources, or operational guidance. Individuals must consult with their compliance department regarding the use of any of the suggested ideas and content. The herein Marketing Calendar is meant to serve as a source of potential ideas only and is not a full complete list of all holidays or events, nor is it meant to be discriminating toward gender, ethnicity, religious observances, or other constituents. Advantus Marketing, LLC, does not guarantee the accuracy of the dates provided, which are generally acknowledged in the US.

CHAPTER 8

HOW TO IMPLEMENT THESE TACTICS TO ACQUIRE CLIENTS & KEEP THEM FOR LIFE

The prescriptive tactics and real-world insights I have shared with you in this book are designed to help you elevate your clients' and prospects' experience and engage with them emotionally to build the relationships that create a sustainable business.

You may have taken particular note of some of the tactics that you want to implement. That is terrific, but at the end of the day, what is the plan? What are the steps you will take to put them into practice?

A proverb commonly heard on Wall Street says it best: "*To know and not to do is just as good as not to know.*"

HOW CAN YOU IMPLEMENT THE THINGS THAT I HAVE SHARED, AS WELL AS THE OTHER IDEAS THAT HAVE OCCURRED TO YOU WHILE READING THIS BOOK?

Given that the cost of acquiring a new client in terms of time, effort, and capital is high, every client you retain increases your return on the overall cost of new business acquisition.

Unfortunately, when you lose a client, you lose not only the ROI on the original cost of acquiring them but also the lifetime value (LTV) of that client and their business with you.

However, in addition to the ROI and LTV that retaining a client delivers, there is another factor to consider here as well.

THAT FACTOR IS WHAT HAPPENS REPUTATIONALLY AND TO REVENUE IF YOU DON'T IMPLEMENT, DON'T ELEVATE, AND DON'T ADOPT SOME OF THESE TACTICS AND INSIGHTS AND YOUR COMPETITORS DO.

Simply put, there is a cost to elevating the client experience—whether you do or you don't.

For those who implement, your clients will become delighted advocates and spend more money and refer more people to you.

I often hear from people looking for advice on what they should do to grow or retain their business. I, of course, am grateful that they reached out and seek my counsel. Interestingly, there are always a few who are unsure of whether to proceed with a strategy or tactic I suggest because of "the effort needed." This not only speaks to their commitment mindset but often their organizational culture.

Culturally, if the focus is primarily on your process or your products and services, you and your colleagues will likewise be more about self and less about putting in the effort needed to elevate and retain the client.

However, by building a culture around continually improving the experiential value you deliver, you and your team will be known as a business that is set apart from all others.

As I mentioned in the introduction, clients and prospects will have an experience with you, your team, and, if you are in leadership, your organization.

And *you* get to decide what that experience will be!

J.K. Rowling—whose first book was rejected by twelve major publishers before she went on to be the first author to become a billionaire—wrote in *Harry Potter and the Chamber of Secrets*, *"It is our choices…that show what we truly are, far more than our abilities."*

I have been speaking at meetings and conferences around the globe for many years.

At those events, I was struck by the incredible number of great ideas shared by so many brilliant practitioners and speakers.

But I have also been struck by the need for step-by-step execution guidance on *how to do* what is recommended to be done. The reason many people don't implement is that they simply don't know how.

Every action needs prescriptive steps to implement successfully. When this is done, the results are amazing. People can and do execute when they know the steps.

Being better is a great message. But you will only become better by knowing and committing to the specific steps you need to take.

Against this backdrop, here are the practical steps you should take to implement the tactics I have shared.

IMPLEMENTATION STEP 1
Craft a vision that defines the experience your clients and prospects will have.

What is your experiential vision for your clients?

What type of experience do you aspire for them to have with you?

This is not the *why* of what you are doing but rather the experience you will deliver and the legacy you will leave.

Jeff Bezos's vision was and is *"to build the most customer-centric company in the world."*

Notice that this isn't a paragraph. It is just a simple, to-the-point sentence that provides strategic guardrails for every decision around the client experience.

It is as simple as the experiential vision of one of my real estate friends: *"For my clients to feel appreciated and treasured."*

Or my CPA, whose experiential vision is: *"I want every client to feel like they are my most important client."*

Reflect on these vision statements and decide: what is yours? Then write it, post it on a wall, communicate about it, and work to make it happen.

IMPLEMENTATION STEP 2
Assess where you are now and where you need to improve.

This step is challenging for many of us, as it requires reflection, detection, and genuine inspection.

It is never easy to say, "I need to improve on this and this and that." And the more successful you are, the harder it sometimes is to even see areas that need improvement. However, being honest about where you are is the only way to get to where you want to be.

Whether you are a business owner, a solo practitioner, part of a team, or leading an organization, the simple assessment tool in this step will help you uncover where you are and areas upon which you can improve.

Your Two-Part Assessment Tool to Craft an Elevated Experience and a Client and Prospect-Centric Culture

(You can download this tool as a Word Document at RichardWeylman.com under the Resource Tab.)

PART ONE

Assess your current experiential culture using the assessment tool below.

a.   If you are a sole practitioner and you are a bit unsure of the right score for one of the items, go ahead and score it, and then ask a trusted client or two what score they would give you and why. This can be very revealing.

b.   If you are part of a team, each of you should complete this assessment individually and then meet and discuss what each of you scored and why. Finally, come to a consensus on the score that best reflects the experience clients have with you as a team. The key word here is consensus, not compromise. Those that run their business via compromise end up with the politics of disagreement damaging the enterprise and everyone's experience.

Rate your current culture in the following areas (1 = This area is virtually un-addressed; 5 = I/We have total focus in and commitment to this area):

	Rarely			Always	
We are driven to build relationships, not just sales	1	2	3	4	5
We have a clear vision of the experience we deliver	1	2	3	4	5
We welcome new clients with gracious curiosity to know them as people, not just as a client	1	2	3	4	5

	Rarely				Always
We continuously ask clients how we can improve their experience with us	1	2	3	4	5
We consistently demonstrate thoughtfulness, caring, kindness, and empathy for prospects, clients, and each other	1	2	3	4	5
We each give back personally through community involvement	1	2	3	4	5
We have a friendly, flexible, and positive environment and attitude about our work on behalf of others	1	2	3	4	5
We consistently provide a unique and elevated client experience	1	2	3	4	5
We use innovation and creativity to boost client advocacy	1	2	3	4	5
We utilize accountability practices and hold each other accountable	1	2	3	4	5
We pay attention to aesthetics (physical space, attire, etc.)	1	2	3	4	5
We have systems and data fields in place to ask about and track client preferences	1	2	3	4	5
We have open and clear communication across all team members	1	2	3	4	5

PART TWO

Select the three areas from the previous list that are the *most important to address now* to elevate your client's experience.

Consider the three areas you listed as...

Tactic 101. The three areas I/we will improve upon first.

1. _____

2. _____

3. _____

IMPLEMENTATION STEP 3

Be honest with yourself—are you willing?

Having worked with hundreds of professionals in many different industries, I have observed that those that succeed at a high level have the following three traits in common. Now that you have identified the initial three areas that need improvement to keep clients from firing you, I encourage you to reflect on these traits. Ask yourself if they apply to you and be honest in your answers.

1. I am *always* looking to improve, and I am *eagerly* seeking new ideas and approaches.

2. I am *willing* and able to make the changes needed *despite* my current approaches or situation.

3. I want advice and an honest *critique* of how I can do things better.

Success does not come naturally; it requires hard work and being a lifelong student of the ways in which you can improve.

Or as my good friend and fellow Hall of Fame Speaker Bill Bachrach says, *"If comfort is your goal, success is not in your future."*

If you answered yes to all three of the traits above, then you are ready to move on to the exciting next step of implementation.

IMPLEMENTATION STEP 4
Create a plan to implement the necessary tactics.

No matter what you are committed to doing, improvement is a process.

Things will improve incrementally if you have a plan and the discipline to follow it.

The good news is that once you have identified the three areas that need the most improvement, you can focus on them. Specifically, you can select the tactics from this book and others from your own experience that will incrementally address those three areas.

Select those that will get you from where you are to where you want to be.

To ensure the tactics that you select get implemented and stay a priority for you, the key is to have a specific, detailed Ninety-Day Plan listing actions, dates, and responsible parties. As a consulting firm with clients in many industries, they have proven that having and working with an incremental Ninety-Day Plan sequentially throughout the year is a win for them. It will be a win for you also, as you not only can track progress but also get to celebrate each completed item. And we like celebrations as much as you do!

A good friend who runs a very large company said to me, *"Richard, I love these sequential Ninety-Day Plans. Every ninety days we craft a new one based upon what we want to improve upon. And the good news is we get more done, and I can also figure out what isn't working faster!"*

Below, I have provided a Ninety-Day Plan template for you to consider, as well as step-by-step guidance on how to use it. (You can download this tool as a Word Document at RichardWeylman.com under the Resource Tab.)

A Ninety-Day Plan enables you to be proactive and execute effectively.

As you create each Ninety-Day Plan, take the following steps:

1. Identify *all* the key tactics for the next ninety days to realize progress in the areas you know you need to improve upon. Be very tactical here. Don't be limited by the template that has space to list only three specific tactics. Use as many pages as you need to list the specific tactics and actions you will be taking. I have some clients that have eighteen to twenty items on their Ninety-Day Plan.

2. Candidly, list the obstacles you will face. This is a very important step. Strategize and work though the obstacles that could prevent you from succeeding. Prioritize to get things done.

3. Detail the action steps and items and log the due dates and your accountability.

4. At the end of each ninety days, assess what you have accomplished and create your next Ninety-Day Plan. This enables you to continue to move ahead with the tactics needed to engage clients emotionally, elevate their experiences, and create a business of distinction.

A Ninety-Day Plan to Elevate the Client Experience by Addressing Areas for Improvement, Actions to Take, and Specific Steps to Move Ahead

Tactic to implement/ action to take	Action steps to proceed (how will I/ we do this?)	Challenges/ obstacles (yours, mine, ours)	Accountability	
			Who is responsible?	Date to implement
1.				
2.				
3.				

IMPLEMENTATION STEP 5
Seek input from peers.

Success-minded people invest in themselves. With so much "try this, try that" noise in the marketplace, from my experience, the best ideas can be found by following these steps.

1.   Create or join a study group of six to eight successful individuals and collaborate every ten to twelve weeks or so on what each of you are doing to stand apart and create an elevated experience culture in your business.

2.   Create a client advisory board of five to seven best clients and meet quarterly for an honest critique and review of how you can improve the experience they and other clients have with you.

3.   Read or listen to two books a month to expand your knowledge.

4.   Identify positive, productive people in your network and seek their counsel.

5.   Connect with and follow those that deliver real, actionable insight into what people are seeking today from professionals.

The wealth of useful ideas you will gain from taking initiative on these steps will be immeasurable.

IMPLEMENTATION STEP 6

Create weekly or daily rituals.

As you continuously become aware of ways to elevate the experience your clients have with you, be sure to codify them.

Many teams and organizations have a list of things they habitually do for clients. However, making consistent elevation of the client experience a part of your culture is not as simple as reading a policy manual or adding the things to do or your expectations to a list.

To ensure that the client experience is at the top of everyone's mind each week, many teams and organizations regularly highlight and discuss one of the things they do to elevate their clients' experience.

Many refer to this as their weekly (or in some cases daily) "ritual." They perform this ritual because they never want to forget that without the client, there is no business.

Moreover, many have told me that the ten minutes they spend together engaged in the ritual is one of the most rewarding parts of their meetings, as it engages everyone. It allows them to get feedback on the item and new tweaks to make it better. You should do the same. But just like cultivating a client, if you don't cultivate a ritual, it does not take long for it to be out of sight, out of mind, and, in this case, out of use.

IMPLEMENTATION STEP 7

Revamp, renew, and be persistent.

If you are the senior leader in a company, to integrate these tactics into your culture you will likely need to revamp some education and training programs. Doing so will help ensure that you and the entire organization deliver a consistently elevated experience. We can assist you with that.

You may even consider doing what several brands have done: They have reorganized and have both the training department and the marketing department reporting to a Chief Customer Officer who has clout and a budget.

Remember, an elevated experience creates emotional chemistry, stronger relationships, repeat business, and brand advocacy for you.

So be persistent in your pursuit and delivery.

Rick DeVos, the cofounder of Amway and former owner of the Orlando Magic basketball team, said of persistence:

IT IS A GOD-GIVEN COMPENSATION FOR WHAT WE LACK IN OTHER AREAS OF OUR LIFE. NEVER UNDERESTIMATE ITS POWER.

Well said.

Finally—let me and others hear from you.

It has been a privilege to share these tactics with you, and I thank you for reading. I know from experience that being kinder, more thoughtful, more empathetic, and more caring will deliver many blessings.

Others will notice, and you will be rewarded and be known for it.

If you enjoyed this book, I would be delighted to hear from you via my email below. And please post a review on Amazon (unless you didn't like it) so others can be encouraged to learn from it.

To inquire about having me speak at your next meeting, annual conference, or association convention, or for consulting or coaching services, please feel welcome to email me at richard@richardweylman.com.

Feel welcome to also visit: www.richardweylman.com. There you can also download under the Resource Tab the various tools in this book as a Word Document to facilitate implementation.

And certainly feel welcome to visit and subscribe to both my YouTube channel: www.youtube.com/@RichardWeylman and my blog: www.richardweylman.com/performance-tips/. Please feel welcome to follow me on LinkedIn and on X as well.

A FINAL THOUGHT TO
KEEP YOU ON THE RIGHT PATH:
"LET US NOT LOSE HEART IN DOING GOOD,
FOR IN DUE TIME WE WILL REAP IF WE DO
NOT GROW WEARY."
—GALATIANS 6:9

Continued blessing and warm regards,
Richard

Please send all other correspondence to our corporate headquarters at

Richard Weylman Inc.
P.O. Box 510970
Punta Gorda, FL 33951

Thank you.

AFTERWORD

Richard Weylman is one of those unique individuals who loves to teach people powerful techniques that change human and business relationships for the better. I expected a great book, but in this prolific book, he has really outperformed his previous great books. I have known Richard for many years. I always admire his ability to articulate the rapidly evolving needs of customers, and how to engage and build relationships with them in the most relevant and effective ways.

What I love most about Richard is that he practices what he teaches. People trust Richard because throughout his career, whether at Rolls Royce or *Robb Report*, and in his entrepreneurial journey, he has always demonstrated his expertise, empathy, trustworthiness, and kindness. Maybe it is because he has always retained his deep desire to grow and excel, and to teach others to do the same. It gives him joy.

This book should be used as your bible for customer relationship strategies and tactics. Chapters that I will use over and over are Chapters 5, 6, and 7. Those are gems chock-full of insights and tactics that will make you very successful in your professional and even your personal life. I wish you good luck. And with Richard's great book your luck will be augmented dramatically—with great skill.

My best regards,
Milton Pedraza
CEO, Luxury Institute, LLC

ACKNOWLEDGMENTS

This book was by no means a solo journey of discovery.

First and foremost, I thank God for his favor and for the words that flowed through me onto these pages.

I am grateful for my wife Sylvie who kept me moving forward with her gentle words of encouragement and prayerful support.

To Rolex, our Australian Labradoodle, who would tolerate my office door being closed only for a few hours and then would bark until I stopped writing and spent time with him. He provided breaks and times of reflection I didn't know I needed until they occurred. And to Tiffany, our Calico cat, who waited patiently for her turn but would cry incessantly if that seemed to be too long as well.

To Deb Nelson, Tiffany Markarian, Lauren Stakutis, Dick Harris, and Kim Kubinski who are wonderful coaches and as a part of my team, were true sounding boards.

To Dianne Wicker, a retired missionary and saint who prayed for me through this journey.

To Randy Peyser, of Author One Stop, Inc. Without her input, guidance, and brilliance this would not be a book in print.

To the clients, friends, and total strangers that elevated the experiences I had with them and their firms that inspired me.

And finally, to Ken Clary of Atlanta, Georgia, whose story is in one of the tactics in this book. Ken has been a dear friend and spiritual dad to me for many years. He is the epitome of a gentleman and one who has exampled that *friend raising precedes fundraising* every day of his professional career of over sixty years. To him I am also forever grateful.

ABOUT THE AUTHOR

Richard (not C. as noted in tactic 1) is a highly sought-after keynote speaker, author, and business growth consultant. He possesses a unique ability to see things from the client's perspective and interpret their needs, putting audience members regardless of industry or role on a proven path for permanent business growth and success.

Inducted into the Professional Speaker Hall of Fame, associations and Fortune 500 companies globally engage Richard to speak at their conferences for his insights and tactics in acquiring and keeping clients/customers for life. His presentations inspire, encourage, and inform audience members with prescriptive strategies and tactics that produce measurable results.

In addition to his induction into the Professional Speaker Hall of Fame, he has also earned a place in the Customer Experience (CX) Hall of Fame for his innovative practices in fostering connections between brands and clients.

He has received many awards and accolades including being a two-time recipient of the *Keynote Presentations Specialist of the Year* (USA) by *Wealth & Finance International Media.*

Additionally, he is recognized by Engati Global as a *Customer Experience Global Influencer.*

He has appeared on dozens of podcasts, radio talk shows, TV segments and on internal corporate networks.

Both of his previous books *Opening Closed Doors: Key to Reaching Hard-to-Reach People* and *The Power of Why: Breaking Out in a Competitive Marketplace* are international bestsellers.

Christopher Forbes, vice chair of Forbes Media, describes Richard Weylman's extraordinary insights and dynamic prescriptive presentations on business growth and creating client/customer advocacy *"brilliant."*

He is the founder of both The Weylman Center for Excellence in Practice Management, an online marketing education platform for financial professionals, as well as Weylman Consulting & Coaching Group, whose client base is in many different sectors of industry such as finance, luxury goods, NFL teams, real estate, and fast casual dining.

With homes in Florida and Hawaii, it was not always that way. Orphaned at age six, Richard lived in nineteen foster homes and attended eleven different schools.

Rather than becoming victim of those circumstances, he overcame them and achieved remarkable business success, including serving as an award-winning general sales manager at Rolls-Royce to heading (leading) sales and marketing for the *Robb Report,* a luxury lifestyle magazine, from its inception until its then-record liquidity event.

Finally, Richard is a *Horatio-Alger* nominee for his continual philanthropic work on behalf of orphans and widows.

Mango Publishing, established in 2014, publishes an eclectic list of books by diverse authors—both new and established voices—on topics ranging from business, personal growth, women's empowerment, LGBTQ studies, health, and spirituality to history, popular culture, time management, decluttering, lifestyle, mental wellness, aging, and sustainable living. We were named 2019 *and* 2020's #1 fastest growing independent publisher by *Publishers Weekly.* Our success is driven by our main goal, which is to publish high-quality books that will entertain readers as well as make a positive difference in their lives.

Our readers are our most important resource; we value your input, suggestions, and ideas. We'd love to hear from you—after all, we are publishing books for you!

Please stay in touch with us and follow us at:

Facebook: Mango Publishing
X: @MangoPublishing
Instagram: @MangoPublishing
LinkedIn: Mango Publishing
Pinterest: Mango Publishing
Newsletter: mangopublishinggroup.com/newsletter

Join us on Mango's journey to reinvent publishing, one book at a time.

Printed in the USA
CPSIA information can be obtained
at www.ICGtesting.com
JSHW031048270224
56402JS00004B/4